"MAKE US A GOD!"

"MAKE US A GOD!"

A JEWISH RESPONSE TO HEBREW CHRISTIANITY

* * *

A SURVIVAL MANUAL FOR JEWS

* * *

- What is Jesus for Jews?
  - Is "Messianic Judaism" Jewish?
    - How to Answer Missionary Arguments

By
CHAIM PICKER

iUniverse, Inc.
New York Lincoln Shanghai

"MAKE US A GOD!"
A JEWISH RESPONSE TO HEBREW CHRISTIANITY
A SURVIVAL MANUAL FOR JEWS

Copyright © 2005 by Chaim Picker

iUniverse books may be ordered through booksellers or by contacting:

iUniverse
2021 Pine Lake Road, Suite 100
Lincoln, NE 68512
www.iuniverse.com
1-800-Authors (1-800-288-4677)

ISBN-13: 978-0-595-36933-1 (pbk)
ISBN-13: 978-0-595-81344-5 (ebk)
ISBN-10: 0-595-36933-2 (pbk)
ISBN-10: 0-595-81344-5 (ebk)

Printed in the United States of America

"Hear, Oh Israel, YHVH is our God, YHVH is One" (Deut. 6:4).

"You shall have no other gods before me" (Exod. 20:3).

"…before me no god was formed neither shall there be after me. I, even I, am YHVH, and beside me there is no savior" (Isa. 43:10-12).

"When the people saw that Moses delayed to come down from the mountain, the people gathered together to Aaron and said to him, 'Up, **make us a god** that shall go before us…'" (Exod. 32:1).

Acknowledgements

The following were indispensable in the technical preparation of my manuscript: Sylvie Golden and Audrie Sturman, for their meticulous proofreading; Robert Miller, who took on the arduous task of digitizing my manuscript; and finally, Dr. Sandor Schuman, without whose computer skills and unstinting friendship this book would not have seen the light of day.

Dedication

For the preservation and perpetuation of my People.

CONTENTS

ABBREVIATIONS

HEBREW SCRIPTURES

Gen.	Genesis	Eccl.	Ecclesiastes
Exod.	Exodus	Song	Song of Solomon
Lev.	Leviticus	Isa.	Isaiah
Num.	Numbers	Jer.	Jeremiah
Deut.	Deuteronomy	Lam.	Lamentations
Josh.	Joshua	Ezek.	Ezekiel
Judg.	Judges	Dan.	Daniel
Ruth	Ruth	Hos.	Hosea
I Sam.	I Samuel	Joel	Joel
II Sam.	II Samuel	Amos	Amos
I Ki.	I Kings	Obad.	Obadiah
II Ki.	II Kings	Jon.	Jonah
I Chron.	I Chronicles	Mic.	Micah
II Chron.	II Chronicles	Nah.	Nahum
Ezra	Ezra	Hab.	Habakkuk
Neh.	Nehemiah	Zeph.	Zephaniah
Est.	Esther	Hag.	Haggai
Job	Job	Zech.	Zechariah
Ps.	Psalms	Mal.	Malachi
Prov.	Proverbs		

CHRISTIAN SCRIPTURES

Mt.	Matthew	I Tim.	I Timothy
Mk.	Mark	II Tim.	II Timothy
Lu.	Luke	Tit.	Titus
Jn.	John	Philem.	Philemon
Acts	Acts	Heb.	Hebrews
Rom.	Romans	Jas.	James
I Cor.	I Corinthians	I Pet.	I Peter
II Cor.	II Corinthians	II Pet.	II Peter
Gal.	Galatians	I Jn.	I John
Eph.	Ephesians	II Jn.	II John
Php.	Phillippians	III Jn.	III John
Col.	Colossians	Jude	Jude
I Thess.	I Thessalonians	Rev.	Revelation
II Thess.	II Thessalonians		

PREFACE

PURPOSE OF THE BOOK

This book is intended for Jews who have accepted Jesus as their messiah and Jews who seek a response to "Hebrew-Christian" missionaries. Although our subtitle is "Hebrew-Christianity," the book treats Christian doctrine in general. "Hebrew-Christianity," as embodied in the modern missionary movements, "Jews for Jesus" and "Messianic Judaism," adheres essentially to traditional Christian theology.

EXPLANATION OF TERMS, "MESSIANIC JUDAISM" AND "YHVH"

Throughout our book, the term "Messianic Judaism" is in quotation marks. Since Jews have entertained a messianic hope for several thousand years, to write "Messianic Jew" without the quotation marks would blur the distinction between traditional Jews who hope for the Messiah and "Hebrew-Christians" who regard Jesus as the messiah.

The most distinctive name for God in the Hebrew Scriptures is the Tetragrammaton—the four Hebrew letters *Yod-Heh-Vav-Heh*. The King James Bible of 1611 renders the Tetragrammaton as "LORD," in all capital letters. We have rendered it as YHVH, to avoid confusion with the "Lord" of the Christian Scriptures. We are aware that this is a sensitive issue for Jews who reverently substitute *Adonai*, "My Lord," or *Hashem*, "The Name," for the ineffable Name. Our readers may choose to pronounce YHVH as "*Yahweh*," or "*Hashem*."

THE AUTHOR'S ORIGINS AND EARLY SEARCH

I am descended from orthodox Jews who emigrated to America in the early twentieth century. As an inquisitive youth, I came under the influence of a Jewish uncle who had become a Christian. Under his gentle and persuasive tutelage, I embraced Christianity…

But the same inquisitive mind which propelled me into Christianity was to be the vehicle for my journey back. My purpose here is to share what I have learned about Judaism and Christianity. When I contemplate my strange odyssey, I think of the Biblical Joseph of old and his reunion with his brothers who had come to Egypt to buy grain during the famine. When the brothers learned that the "lord of the land" was their brother Joseph, they were fearful. To assuage their guilt and set them at ease, Joseph assured them: "God sent me before you to preserve a remnant for you on earth…So it was not you who sent me here but God (Gen. 45:5-8). Like Joseph, I sense a purpose in my strange odyssey and believe it has prepared me for a unique mission to my fellow Jews. My return to Judaism was not an easy path. There were many agonizing questions. I invite you now to share with me what I have learned.

Chaim Picker
Albany, New York
August, 16, 2005

INTRODUCTION

JUDAISM NOT A MISSIONARY RELIGION

Judaism is not a missionary religion. It does not actively seek converts and does not require that one be a Jew to be blessed of God. The rabbis teach: "The righteous Gentile has a share in the world to come" (Tosefta, Sanhedrin 13). This sentiment is also echoed in the prophets: "Have we not all one father?" (Mal. 2:10). "Let all peoples walk each in the name of its god, but we will walk in the name of YHVH our God forever" (Mic. 4:5). While adhering fervently to its monotheistic faith, Judaism respects the faiths of others. This book attempts to demonstrate that Judaism and Christianity have significant, non-negotiable differences and explains why Jews cannot accept Jesus as the Messiah. It further encourages Jews who have become Christians to return to their ancestral faith .

CONVERTS TO CHRISTIANITY KNOW LITTLE ABOUT JUDAISM

Most Jewish converts to Christianity are not knowledgeable about Judaism. Typically, their Jewish education ended at the age of thirteen, upon becoming a *Bar-or Bat-Mitzvah*—the Jewish ceremony for attaining the age of responsibility. Before considering conversion, we urge our fellow Jews to examine from authentic Jewish sources the richness of their 3500-year-old heritage. Unfortunately, this rarely occurs. When a Jew becomes a Christian, the new faith is studied with far greater diligence than was devoted to the ancestral faith. It may occur that the new convert will seek to reinvestigate his former faith. However, because the motivation is to become a more effective missionary to fellow Jews, objectivity often is lacking.

FAITH AND REASON

In a discussion with a "Hebrew-Christian," we were told: "My belief is personal and not subject to theological debate. No argument can dissuade me from my belief in Jesus! If one has the holy spirit, there is no turning back. One must have the faith of a little child." If a Jew had responded in the above manner, he would have been criticized for giving in to emotionalism.

A "messianic" tract entitled, "Yeshua, who is he?", asks: "Is Jesus the Jewish Messiah, the savior of the world? If he is, let us follow him. If he is not, let us

1

expose him, for only the truth will set us free." Thus, when the *missionary* initiates the action, "theological debate" and logical reasoning are acceptable. We assume that by "truth" the tract intends the Hebrew Scriptures. When Jesus said, "Your word is truth" (Jn. 17:17), he obviously meant the Hebrew Scriptures, the only ones available to him (Luke 4:1; 24:27). When Paul spoke of "Scripture" (II Tim. 3:16), he likewise meant the Hebrew Scriptures. We, then, for our part, will appeal primarily to the Hebrew Scriptures to support our position.

"SHUN DEBATE"—PAUL

After countless dialogues with "Hebrew-Christians," we have come to believe that religious belief usually is a matter of the heart rather than the intellect. The philosopher William James said, "If your heart does not want, your head will assuredly never make you believe." Paul discouraged debate: "Have nothing to do with stupid, senseless controversies; you know they breed quarrels" (II Tim. 2:23; I Tim. 6:3–5, 20; I Cor. 2:l,2; II Tim. 2:l4; Tit. 3:9).

When the cherished beliefs of "Messianic Jews" are refuted by Scripture, some typical responses are: "Without the spirit's anointing there can be no true understanding." Or, "There are mysteries which must be accepted on faith." But let a Jew answer in this vein and he will be accused of being evasive!

Notwithstanding, Jesus and Paul quote Scripture and engage in dialectics! (Luke 24:27; cf. Acts 17:11; Rom. 15:4; II Tim. 3:16). We, for our part, will do the same.

JEWS SHOULD KNOW HOW TO ANSWER

To avoid offending Christians, some Jews may be uncomfortable with a book that challenges Christian teachings. Considering the current ecumenical mood, most Jews would rather avoid controversy. But Jews should not be timid about defending their beliefs. The Tanna Rabbi Elazar taught: "Know how to answer an apostate" (*Aboth* 2:19). The Psalmist said: "I will speak of Your testimonies also before kings, and I will not be ashamed" (Ps. 119:46). We claim the same right as Paul, who said: "Be ready always to give an answer..." (I Pet. 3:15). Isaiah said our criterion should be "the Law and the Testimony" (Isa. 8:20). In the manner of Jesus and Paul, who based their teachings on the Hebrew Scriptures, we shall judge the teachings of Christianity by those same Scriptures.

One should not fear to have one's beliefs scrutinized: "We can do nothing against the truth, but only for the truth" (II Cor 13:8; cf. Jn. 3:21). To those whom this book may offend, we say with Paul: "Am I therefore become your enemy, because I tell you the truth?" (Gal. 4:16).

OUR APPROACH TO BIBLE STUDY

The Hebrew Scriptures constitute a veritable library, written by many hands, over many centuries. One probably could find support in its pages for virtually any theory. To validate a teaching, therefore, one should seek for *persistent* themes rather than isolated passages. Accordingly, we have quoted copiously from various books of the Bible. Since our quotations often are isolated from their source, we urge our readers to open their Bibles and examine the context. We concur with Paul who said, "No prophecy of Scripture is a matter of private interpretation" (II Pet. 1:20). Missionaries speak of "the whole counsel of God" (Acts 20:27), implying that one should not rely on "stray" quotations but on a *preponderance* of scriptural evidence (Deut. 8:3; Mt. 4:4). Our book adheres to this principle.

*   *   *

To our Jewish brothers and sisters who have accepted the Christian messiah, we say with heartfelt conviction: Come and reason with us. Re-examine your ancestral faith with the same diligence you have devoted to your new-found faith: "If you seek her as silver and search for her as for hid treasures, then shall you understand the fear of YHVH and find the knowledge of God" (Prov. 3:5–8; 2:4,5).

"THE HIGHEST REGARD FOR TRUTH IS NOT TO PROFESS IT
BUT TO SEEK FOR IT"
(Edward Westermarck, *Christianity and Morals*).

CHAPTER I

"HEBREW CHRISTIANITY" AND THE MISSIONIZING OF JEWS

"SAVING JEWISH SOULS"

To win a Jew for Christ has ever been a cherished goal of Christian missionaries. What accounts for this obsession to convert Jews? Is it the "saving" of Jewish souls? While this may impel some zealous Christians, we would suggest a deeper motivation. The continued existence of the Jew is an embarrassment to Christianity. Having rejected the "messiah, savior of the world," and being held responsible for the death of the "incarnate god," Jews ought not to be flourishing and spiritually viable. Rather, the "accursed" Jews ought to be in a wretched state! The conversion of the Jew, therefore, is seen as a validation of the Christian faith.

SUBTLE TACTICS REPLACE FORCED CONVERSIONS

For centuries, forced conversions were used against Jews, the most infamous example of which was the Spanish Inquisition. In medieval Europe, Jews were burned at the stake—*auto-da-fe*, ("act of faith"). Incredibly, this fiendish practice was justified from Christian Scripture: "If any man's work is burned up, he will suffer loss, though he himself will be saved, but only as through fire...You are to deliver such a one to Satan for the destruction of the flesh, that his spirit may be saved in the day of the Lord Jesus" (I Cor. 3:15; 5:5). Blind, religious fanatics believed that burning the body of the "infidel" Jew would save his soul! This heinous deed was considered meritorious—an "act of faith." Forced, cruel conversions eventually gave way to more sophisticated missionary tactics, conceived by apostate Jews. Special missions to Jews were established, with converted Jews as the principal agents to missionize their fellow Jews. Today, the most active of these missionary endeavors are "Jews for Jesus," and "Messianic Judaism."

"RESTORING THE JEWISHNESS OF JESUS"

There are two movements to "restore the Jewishness of Jesus"—one sincere, the other sinister. Enlightened Christians are scandalized by the disenfranchisement of the Jew and his century-old persecution by the Church. Believing it to be immoral and unscriptural, they seek brotherhood and equality with Jews and the elimination of anti-Semitism. "Messianic Jews," on the other hand, seek the *conversion* of Jews. For the latter, emphasizing the "Jewishness" of Jesus is intended to lure Jews to Christianity.

Being strongly nationalistic and having suffered endless persecution, Jews grow defensive when they perceive a threat to their heritage or sense an attempt to induce them to betray their people. To counter these tendencies Jews are told that accepting Christ is not forfeiting Jewishness but is a "return to pristine Judaism." Witness the following testimony of a convert:

"I did not feel pride toward my Jewishness until I became a believer in the Messiah of Israel. Jesus has made me more Jewish than ever. We are not 'converted' but 'completed' Jews! We have not merged with the Gentile majority but remain distinctly Jewish."

"Hebrew-Christian" missionaries take their cue from Christianity's master soul-winner, Paul. His missionary-strategy was, "To the Jew I became as a Jew" (I Cor. 9:20,22; 10:32, 33). Thus, Paul acted "Jewish" when Paul dealt with Jews. Paul's modern-day disciples likewise affect an appearance of "Jewishness," adopting "Jewish" symbols and terminology: The Hebrew Scriptures are the *Tanach*; Jesus is *Yeshua Ha Mashiach*; the New Testament is the *Brit Chadasha*. A new, "messianic" translation of the Christian Scriptures, the *Jewish New Testament,* utilizes Hebraisms: Matthew is *"Matithyahu,"* John is *"Yochanan,"* the disciples are *"talmidim,"* Paul is *"Shaul,"* etc.

Franz Delitzsch, a leading 19th-century German Christian theologian, candidly admitted he had mastered Hebrew in order to more effectively missionize Jews. Indeed, one wonders whether today's "Messianic Jews" study Hebrew for the same reason.

TARGETING THE VULNERABLE

Certain individuals are vulnerable to missionaries. The lonely and alienated find solace in Christianity's message. Indeed, Christianity's demands may appear less stringent than those of Judaism. Paul calls the Law "a yoke of slavery" (Gal. 5:1; cf. Mt. 23:4). Jesus promised: "The truth shall make you free!" (Jn. 8:32). Israel's God is portrayed as distant and abstract whereas Jesus is more personal and accessible. Christians are encouraged to come to him with child-like trust (Mt. 18:3).

Zealous missionaries do not shrink from proselytizing even the young, fortified by Jesus' words: "I have come to set a man against his father, and a daughter against her mother...He who loves father or mother more than me is not worthy of me" (Mt. l0:34–37; Lu. 9:59, 60; Mt. 12:48). This practice often divides families, causing pain and anguish. Missionaries should consider the Torah's injunction: "You shall not put a stumbling block before the blind" (Lev. 19:14). In this vein, the Talmud wisely cautions: "If you wish to give a child food, first tell its mother" (Simeon b. Gamliel II, Talm. Shab. 10b).

The following story is an example of outrageous and unabashed missionary zeal. A "Messianic Jew" invited us to accompany her on a visit to an elderly Jewish patient in the hospital next to the synagogue. She brought him flowers and spoke soothingly and comfortingly to him as he lay in his hospital bed, a kippah on his head. Before departing, she uttered a prayer that he might receive "*Yeshua Hamashiach*" (Messiah Jesus). Although we were deeply offended and pained, but not wanting to upset the elderly gentleman, we said nothing but proceeded to offer a Hebrew prayer for his speedy recovery. Outside the hospital, we spoke to our "Messianic-Jewish" friend:

"We commend you for visiting and comforting the sick. But it is wrong to evangelize the elderly Jew, taking advantage of one in a weakened condition who does not fully grasp what you are doing. You have violated the scriptural injunction of "putting a stumbling block before the blind."

"But I don't want him to die unsaved!" replied our friend.

We countered: "This is sheer arrogance—this presumption of yours that he is unsaved because he has not accepted your 'Yeshua'! We are weary of hearing that Jews are damned, whereas believers in Jesus are saved. Preach to *us*, if you will, for we can answer you. But do not ply your missionary tactics against the defenseless!"

MODERN MISSIONARIES LIKE THE ANCIENT AMALEKITES

The missionary tactics of targeting "stragglers"—the love-starved, alienated, aged and young—are reminiscent of the ancient Amalekites: "Remember what Amalek did to you on the way as you came out of Egypt, how he attacked you on the way when you were faint and weary, and cut off at your rear all who lagged behind you; and he did not fear God" (Deut. 25:17,18). The modern

"Amalekites" are wolves in sheep's clothing, who prey on the Jewish flock and hunt Jewish souls (Ezek. 13:18).

NEW "STATUS" OF JEWISH CONVERTS

When the Jew enters the Christian fold, he is joyfully embraced as one of God's chosen people. Given the "mystique" surrounding the Jew, he often becomes a celebrity. Invariably, with characteristic Jewish diligence, he rises to leadership among Christians, garnering much ego-satisfaction.

"CHRISTIAN LOVE"

Prospective Jewish converts are told how much "Jews are loved." A famous leader of the Protestant Reformation at first expressed great love for the Jews—until he realized Jews were poor clients for conversion. Then his "love" turned to virulent hatred. We were reminded of this during a discussion with a "Messianic Jew." Initially, there were fulsome expressions of "love" for the Jews. When stereotypical missionary arguments began to wither under the scrutiny of Scripture, our disputant's manner grew harsher and we were told, "Jews are devoid of God's spirit." We wondered how long it would be before we heard the words, "Jews are accursed"—or even, Jews are a "synagogue of Satan" (Rev. 2:9).

"MESSIANIC CONGREGATIONS"

"Messianic Jews," not feeling at home in the traditional churches, form their own congregations, holding services on the Sabbath. We attended one such "messianic" synagogue on a Friday evening and were exposed to a strange amalgam of "Jewish" and Christian motifs. There was an *aron kodesh* (Torah ark) and a "Torah desk" with a Star of David. On the ark were the words, "Yeshua [Jesus], the Light of the World." A Torah scroll was taken out and the "rabbi," wearing a *tallit* (prayer-shawl), proudly declared that the scroll was over a hundred years old. The rabbi haltingly read a few lines from the scroll, his garbled pronunciation betraying his deficiency in Hebrew. As we contemplated how this venerable old Torah scroll, once lovingly and piously kept by a Jewish congregation, was now serving as an "amulet" in a Christian setting, we were pained. The mock Torah-service was followed by the lighting of Sabbath candles, blessing over the wine-cup and Sabbath loaves, singing of Jewish-sounding hymns, and Israeli dancing. The catchword *"Yeshua-Mashiach"* was pervasive. Introducing the "guest-rabbi" the evening's scheduled speaker, the host-rabbi smilingly related how he had taken his guest to a restaurant that afternoon, where he was treated to the town's famed "cheese-steak." While this evoked laughter from the congregation, we were saddened at this flippant disregard for the dietary laws, inscribed in the very Torah that had just been so ceremoniously handled. Listening to the "guest-rabbi" preach, we were particularly struck by the pains he took to prove it was all "Jewish"—Jesus was a good Jewish boy; the apostles were Jews; the New Testament was a Jewish book, etc. We could not repress the feeling that his protestations only betrayed his insecurity as to his own "Jewishness."

A "Messianic Jew" may wear a *Magen-David* ("Star of David") and utilize Hebrew, Jewish symbols, and Jewish ceremonies. But all this is a charade. If he believes that "God became flesh" (Jn. 1:1,14), he has denied Hebrew monotheism. If he prays "in the name of *Yeshua Ha-Mashiach*," he has gone against biblical faith: "Whom have I in heaven but you?" (73:25). "Beside me there is no savior" (Isa. 43:11).

"CHRISTIAN SALVATION"—DEATH FOR JEWS

Referring to his former countrymen, Paul said: "Brothers, my heart's desire and prayer to God for Israel is that they might be saved" (Rom. 10:1). Ironically, the "salvation" that Paul would visit on the Jews is DEATH! The hundreds of thousands of Jews who embraced Christ over the centuries have been lost to our people. They have no Jewish descendants!

The following dedicatory appeared in a missionary book: "For the glory of the God of Abraham, Isaac and Jacob—for the blessing of Abraham's children who still wait for the salvation of Israel." But Hebrew Christianity is not a blessing for Abraham's children. It effectively wipes out their ancestral heritage. Descendants of Hebrew Christians are invariably absorbed into the Gentile-Christian world.

Although "Hebrew-Christians" affect the Star of David, a more appropriate symbol would be the crucifix, for Paul said: "I am determined to know nothing more among you save Jesus Christ and him crucified" (I Cor. 2:2). Hebrew Christians greet us with "*Shalom*"—"Peace"; but their work is for our destruction! Concerning them the prophet declares: "They have healed the wound of my people lightly, saying, 'Peace, peace,' when there is no peace" (Jer. 6:14; 8:11).

"HEBREW-CHRISTIANS" NOT JEWISH

A missionary tract declares: "Jesus was Jewish! He never converted to anything!" This is a gross deception. Jesus' birth is irrelevant. The issue is not birth but *belief*. Hebrew-Christians believe Jesus was the Messiah-Savior, the incarnation of God. They are not Jewish but *Christian*.

"HEBREW-CHRISTIANITY"—A SPIRITUAL HOLOCAUST

A missionary tract contains a drawing entitled, "The Indestructible Jew—He has stood by the grave of every oppressor." The drawing depicts graves of the "oppressors" of Jews through the ages. Standing over one open, unmarked grave, a Jew asks, "Who next?" Sadly, we must answer, "All the Jewish converts through the centuries," for conversion to Christianity is certain spiritual death for Jews. These converts perished to our people. Their descendants are Christians who have disappeared into the Christian-Gentile world.

The "Hebrew-Christians" may comfort themselves with assurances of the indestructibility of the Jewish People but they should ask themselves: "What if all Jews followed their example?" Surely, "Hebrew-Christianity" is a spiritual holocaust for the Jewish People.

"MY OWN VINEYARD HAVE I NOT KEPT"

In a conversation with a "Hebrew-Christian," we were told: "Jews have suffered much in the last 1900 years in the name of Christ. We are dedicated to counteracting anti-Semitism in the churches, undoing the holocaust." We replied: "Solomon's words apply to you: 'My own vineyard have I not kept' (Song 1:6). You would be better advised to strengthen your fellow Jews in their *Judaism.*"

"A JEW IS ONE WHO HAS JEWISH GRANDCHILDREN"

To what avail is it when a converted Jew protests his continued "Jewishness"? It is like mixing wine and water: The wine-taste may linger; but as the diluted wine is repeatedly mixed with water, the wine-taste gradually disappears. Thus, after a few generations, descendants of Jewish converts lose their Jewish identity. Someone wisely observed: "A Jew is one who has Jewish grandchildren!"

A young Jew, who was being influenced by Hebrew Christian missionaries, made the following criticism: "Judaism is a body without a soul. The synagogue is devoid of feeling. Jews practice empty rituals and pray in a strange tongue. They go through the motions but have no real encounter with God." We replied to our young critic: "The problem is not with Jews or the synagogue; it is with *you!* One will find in the synagogue only what is already in one's heart. God's presence is not defined by physical boundaries. Your judgment of your fellow Jews is too harsh. You should not attempt to judge a person's heart!"

During a morning synagogue-service, an incident occurred that evoked the memory of the above conversation. An elderly gentleman had entered and begun to pray in the mechanical style of one accustomed to repeating the same prayers since his youth. His eyes never lowered to the pages of his prayer book. As we beheld this elderly worshiper, devoutly repeating the prayers from memory, we thought about the criticism of our young Jewish friend. Respect welled up within us for this aged Jew who had been faithful to his heritage for a lifetime. We were transported to another time, perhaps a little *"shtetel"* in Europe, where we envisioned a little boy sitting next to his father in the synagogue, learning the prayers by rote.

"REMOVE NOT THE ANCIENT LANDMARK"

Like the venerable old Jew, Judaism too is old. It is easy to grow impatient and critical…but "love covers a multitude of defects" (Prov. 10:12). Solomon wrote, "A faithful friend loves at all times" (Prov. 17:17). The Psalmist prayed, "Cast me not off in the time of old age" Ps. 71:9). It is easy to criticize a religion four-thousand years old. Sometimes Judaism may become "routinized," but its lovers cherish it. To them it holds a priceless charm, like the warm patina of heirloom furniture. We should not be too quick to "remove the ancient landmark" (Prov. 22:28; 23:10), our ancestral heritage.

"BE NOT RIGHTEOUS OVERMUCH"

The criticism is heard that Jewish formal prayer discourages spontaneity. Admittedly, prescribed prayer tends to become mechanical. On the other hand, the pious prayers of ancient teachers can inspire heartfelt feeling. Many Jewish prayers are from the Psalms and other Scriptures. Prescribed prayer is a unifying force, linking Jews in time and space. The Mishnah, however, cautions: "When you pray, let not your prayer become perfunctory" (*Aboth* 2:18). We are encouraged to add original, personal prayers. "Spontaneous" prayer, as practiced by fundamental Christians, is no guarantee of spirituality. Hypocrites are adept at pious-sounding prayer. Isaiah said: "They honor me with their lips but their heart is far from me" (Isa. 29:13). If one is averse to praying in a "strange tongue," there are options: one may read the English translation, or one may learn Hebrew. Just as one expends energy to prepare for a career, one should be willing to make a similar effort to become literate in the ancient tongue. It is meritorious to pray in the language of our ancestors and our sacred literary treasure, the *Tanach*.

A missionary tract sarcastically accuses Jews of being "more concerned about a kosher stomach than a kosher heart!" Have these glib critics forgotten that the dietary laws were given to Israel by God to make them holy (Lev. 11:44)? One can have a "kosher stomach" *and* a "kosher heart."

To criticize Jews as unfeeling and engaging in meaningless rituals, smacks of self-righteousness. Scripture cautions, "Be not righteous overmuch" (Eccl. 7:16).

Ritual and ceremony *can* evoke spirituality. Man is mind *and* body; ideals are not easily conveyed in a vacuum. Ritual, as an "audio-visual" aid, can help create a religious mood.

Piety is not the sole possession of born-again Christians. Jews also experience the presence of God. In many synagogues, the following is inscribed: "I have set YHVH always before me. Because He is at my right hand, I shall not be moved" (Ps. 16:8).

It is claimed the Jewish God is aloof. To the contrary, the God of Israel is accessible, with no mediator needed to approach Him: "YHVH is near to all who call upon Him, to all who call upon Him in truth" (Ps. 145:18).

Jews are accused of "following rabbinic Judaism," of "substituting the Talmud for Scripture." The Talmud is not a substitution for Scripture, but a commentary on it. It is a testimony to the Jewish love and reverence for Scripture. Jews could make the counter-charge that the Christian Scriptures, with their pagan doctrines of Incarnation and a god co-habiting with a human, are an unwarranted addition to Scripture. And what of the vast body of commentaries that has grown up around the Christian Scriptures—a Christian "talmud," as it were? As for the charge that Jews follow rabbinic Judaism, this is a strange criticism coming from those who call their ministers "rabbis"! Are not "Messianic Jews" following the interpretations of *their* teachers? If they insist they are following the Bible, we reply that we too are following the Bible, as taught to us by our rabbinical teachers. Just as they revere their teachers, we revere ours. Let us not focus on the *teacher* but on his *teachings*: The criterion should be: Is the teaching in harmony with Scripture?

A tract asks, "Who is a Jew?" and arrogantly replies, "Every Jew makes his own religion!" But what of the thousand or more denominations and sects in Christendom, many of whom claim to be "the true and original version"? Even among "Hebrew-Christian" groups, doctrinal differences have cropped up, one group criticizing the other of "heresy" in trying to be too "Jewish." The above-mentioned tract defines "Jew" (Heb. *Yehudi*) as "praiser of God." This is not accurate. It means, "praiser of *Yah* (*Yahweh*)." Are "Messianic Jews" praisers of *Yahweh*—or *Yeshua-Jesus*?

The tract lists "14 facts every Jew should know and believe concerning the Messiah" and gives "proof-texts." All the familiar "messianic prophecies" are mentioned—but one is missing: the "Second Coming." Where in Hebrew Scripture is the prophecy that Messiah would come a second time, thousands of years after his first coming, to complete his mission? We have yet to discover such a reference.

NOT JEWS—NOT CHRISTIANS

"Hebrew-Christians" call themselves "Messianic Jews." In actuality, Judaism is essentially "messianic," that is, it believes in the coming of the Messiah. Where Jews differ, however, is in the *nature* of the Messiah and the *timing* of his coming. The doctrine that the Christian Messiah is co-equal with God, is contrary to Hebrew Scripture (Exod. 20:2,3; Deut. 4:39; 6:4; Isa. 44:6, 8, etc.) Moreover, Messiah's coming is accompanied by universal peace. This has not yet occurred. [Cf. Isa. 9:7; Deut. 18:21,22.]

Chastising those who wavered between the worship of the true God and Baal, the prophet Elijah said: "How long will you halt between two opinions?" (I Ki. 18:21). The Psalmist said: "I hate double-minded men" (119:113). Modern-day "Hebrew-Christians" endeavor to be both Jewish and Christian—an irreconcilable position!

In the early 1970s, "Jews for Jesus" held a rally in New York City. The press reported the following encounter between a woman and one of the group's representatives:

"So which one are you?" the woman in the elevator at the Statler Hilton asked the young man whose jacket was emblazoned with a cross inside a star of David. "I'm both!" he replied. "It is possible to be both!" Accompanying the newspaper article was a photo of the group's leader wearing a Jewish *yarlmuke* (religious head-covering) and religious fringes.

For a "Jew for Jesus" to affect the religious fringes is a self-contradiction: the fringes symbolize the Mosaic Law (Num. 15:37–39), which Christianity disavows (Rom. 6:14)! Endeavoring to retain the dual identity of Jew and Christian is in conflict with Paul: "Neither circumcision counts for anything nor uncircumcision, but a new creation" (Gal. 6:15; II Cor. 5:16,17) . A tract by "Jews for Jesus" states: "We love the holidays…We desire to remain within the Jewish community." But Paul rebukes Jewish "believers" who would observe the Mosaic holidays: "You observe days, and months and seasons and years! I am afraid I have labored over you in vain" (Gal. 4:9,10). Paul calls it a "returning to the weak and beggarly elements." The establishment of separate "Hebrew-Christian" congregations also is contrary to Paul: "For [Christ] is our peace, who has made us both one, and has broken down the dividing wall of hostility by abolishing in his flesh the law of commandments and ordinances, that he might create in himself one new man in place of the two" (Eph. 2:14,15). It is also contradictory for "Hebrew-Christians" to affect Hebrew names, unlike Paul who abandoned his Hebrew name Saul for the Roman name Paul. One wonders why "Messianic Jews" shy away from the name "Christian." Perhaps they do so in their zeal to appear more "Jewish" to Jews. Indeed, Arnold Fruchtenbaum, a leading spokesman for "Hebrew Christianity," calls their position "extreme" (*Hebrew Christianity*, p. 50.) Apparently, they have overlooked Peter's exhortation: "If one suffers as a Christian, let him not be ashamed, *but under that name*, let him glorify God" (I Pet. 4:16). A Christian publication, dedicated to "Jewish Evangelism," expressed concern over the trend in "Messianic Judaism" to incorporate Jewish customs and ceremonies. It compared it to the longing of the freed Israelites for the dainty victuals of Egypt (Num. 11:5). Quoting Gal. 3:13, that "Christ redeemed us from the curse of the law," it warned that the "yearning to return to the old ways" could degenerate into "doctrinal heresy."

SEEDS OF ANTI-SEMITISM

When confronted with the history of Christendom, written with the blood of Jews, the Hebrew-Christian protests: "But they [the persecutors] were not true Christians!" Notwithstanding, the seeds of anti-Semitism are deep within Christianity. (See chapter 17, "Anti-Semitism and the Christian Scriptures.") The Christian dogma of "exclusive salvation" gave rise to the crimes of Christendom against "unbelievers": "He that believes not the son shall not see life but the wrath of God abides upon him" (Jn. 3:16). The faithful believed they were acting as God's messengers when they fought against "unbelievers." The doctrine of "exclusive salvation" breeds intolerance and hatred.

"THE SOUND OF SINGING"

The movement of "Messianic Judaism" is patterned after Pentecostalism, with its enthusiastic singing, dancing, healings and "speaking in tongues." One cannot help but be impressed by the joy of the worshipers. In fact, one might experience a little jealousy and wish that such joyful expression were more in evidence in the rather solemn services of the Synagogue. Admittedly, there *is* a certain seductiveness about the worship-services of "Messianic Jews." We are reminded of the golden-calf episode in Exodus 32. When Moses was descending Sinai with the two tablets, Joshua said to Moses, "There is a noise of war in the camp." Moses replied, "It is not the sound of shouting for victory, or the sound of the cry of defeat, *but the sound of singing* I hear.'" (Exod. 32:15-19). For all its joy and apparent sincerity, the singing of "Messianic Jews" is a funeral dirge for Judaism.

"REJOICE IN THE WIFE OF YOUR YOUTH!"

The Psalmist wrote: "YHVH, I love the habitation of your house…Blessed are those who dwell in your house" (Ps. 26:8; 84:4; cf. Num. 24:5). Hebrew-Christians dwell in a "stranger's" house. It is not the House of Israel. They have gone astray after an alien lover and played the harlot (Jer. ch. 3). They have "taken their idols into their hearts" (Ezek. 14:3,4,7). To them apply the Sage's words: "Rejoice in the wife of your youth…Drink waters out of your own cistern" (Prov. 5:18,15). "Hebrew Christians" have imitated the ancient Israelites who lapsed into idolatry and against whom Jeremiah inveighed: "Has a nation changed its gods, even though they are no gods? But my people have changed their glory for that which does not profit…They have forsaken me, the fountain of living waters, and hewed out cisterns for themselves, broken cisterns that can hold no water" (Jer. 2:11,13).

Aaron's sons, Nadab and Abihu, "offered strange fire before YHVH, which he had not commanded." For this they were punished and YHVH said: "I will be sanctified by those who are near me" (Lev. 10:1-3). In espousing the triune god of Christianity, "Hebrew—Christians" are offering "strange fire" before God, thereby distancing themselves from him. He will not be sanctified by them!

Isaiah wrote: "As for me, this is my covenant with them, says YHVH: my spirit that is upon you, and my words which I have put in your mouth, shall not depart out of your mouth, nor out of the mouth of your seed, nor out of the mouth of your seed's seed, says YHVH, from henceforth and forever" (Isa. 59:20,21). The covenant with Israel is eternal, never to pass away or be replaced by a so-called "new covenant." Jews who embrace Christianity have broken with the ancient covenant. Its sacred words will surely not be found in the mouths of their descendants. "Hebrew-Christians" should heed Isaiah's entreaty: "Look to the Rock from which you were hewn" (Isa. 51:1).

*   *   *

Jews are an endangered species, just as much as elephants, whales, seals and other life-forms. The Jewish heritage is at risk from "Hebrew-Christianity."

CHAPTER 2

GOD IS ONE, NOT THREE

A fundamental theme of the Hebrew Scriptures is MONOTHEISM, the belief in *one, exclusive* God. This is the cardinal teaching of Judaism, as enunciated in Judaism's most sacred dictum, the *Shema*: "Hear, O Israel, YHVH is our God, YHVH is one" (Deut. 6:4). Over against this teaching is the Christian TRINITY, as enunciated in the most ancient and authoritative creeds of the Catholic Church: "The divinity of the Father, and of the Son, and of the Holy Spirit, is one, the glory equal, the majesty co-eternal" (Athanasian Creed, fifth century). The Nicene Creed (fourth century) declares Jesus to be "true God of true God." According to the "Statement of Faith of the Messianic Jewish Alliance, "[God] exists forever in three persons, God the Father, God the Son, and God the Holy Spirit." The Baltimore Catechism states: "We cannot fully understand how the three Divine Persons are one and the same God, because this is a mystery."

But one plus one plus one does not equal one. Trinitarians answer by claiming the Trinity is a "mystery" that must be accepted on faith. It is through such theological sophistries that unbiblical teachings have found their way into Christendom.

If the Trinity is such an important doctrine, why is Scripture so reticent about it? Why is the Trinity a "mystery" that must be *unearthed* from obscure texts by tortuous exegesis? Moreover, almost all the Christian Scripture proof-texts concern the "Father and the Son," rarely the "Holy Spirit," and the word "Trinity" *never* occurs in the Christian Scriptures! The UNITY of God, however, is an explicit and ever-recurring theme in the Hebrew Scriptures!

"PROOF TEXTS" FOR TRINITY

Trinitarians cite the following "proof texts": "And when Jesus was baptized, he went up immediately from the water, and behold, the heavens were opened and he saw the spirit of God descending like a dove, and alighting on him" (Mt. 3:16). [The mere mention of three entities does not equal "Trinity," or "co-equality."] "Go therefore and make disciples of all nations, baptizing them in the name of the Father and of the Son and of the Holy Spirit…" [Mt. 28:19) [Again, no co-equality."] "The grace of the Lord Jesus Christ and the love of God and the fellowship of the Holy Spirit be with you all" (II Cor. 13:14): [Only one of the three is called "God," whereas the Trinity declares that *each one* is "God"!]

Paul comes very close to a creed in Ephesians 4:4-6: "There is one body and one spirit…one Lord, one faith, one baptism, one God and Father of us all, who is above all and through all and in all." Paul's statement is remarkable for two reasons: This would have been the appropriate location for proclaiming the Trinity but there is not even a hint of it! Moreover, Paul unequivocally teaches the supremacy of God: "above all, through all, in all."

GOD'S ONENESS CONFIRMED BY HEBREW SCRIPTURE

Whereas theologians are hard-pressed to substantiate the Trinity scripturally, the ONENESS of God is a recurrent theme in Hebrew Scripture, its paramount importance being demonstrated by its appearance at the head of the Ten Commandments:

"*I* am YHVH your God…You shall have no other gods beside me" (Exod. 20:2,3; 34:14; Deut. 5:7). We have emphasized "I" because of the Hebrew intensive pronoun *anochi*, "I," not *another!* (Cf. Exod. 3:6, 11,12,13; 4:11,) No amount of ingenious interpretations can alter God's own declaration of His ONENESS.

The following passages testify to the Unity of God: [We have left the Hebrew tetragrammaton YHVH untranslated. Most English translations represent it by LORD in capital letters.]

"Hear, O Israel: YHVH our God, YHVH is one" (Deut. 6:4). "YHVH is God; there is no other beside him…YHVH is GOD in heaven above and on earth beneath; there is no other" (Deut. 4:35,39). "Who is like you among the gods, O YHVH?" (Exod. 15:11). "YHVH is greater than all gods" (Exod. 18:11). "Make no mention of the names of other gods, nor let such be heard out of your mouth" (Exod. 23:13). "For what God is there in heaven or on earth who can do such works and mighty acts as these?" (Deut. 3:24). "I, even I, am he, and there is no god beside me" (Deut. 32:39). "For YHVH your God, he is God of gods and Lord of lords, the great, the mighty, and the awesome God" (Deut. 10:17). "For YHVH your God—he is God in heaven above and on earth beneath" (Josh. 2:11). "There is none holy like YHVH, for there is none besides you; and there is no rock like our God" (I Sam. 2:2; II Sam. 7:22; I Chron. 17:20; II Sam. 22:32). "YHVH is God; there is no other" (I Ki. 8:60).

"YHVH, He is God; YHVH, He is God" (I Ki. 18:39). "There is no God in all the earth but in Israel" (II Ki. 5:15). "You are the God, you alone" (II Ki. 19:15,19). "Yours, YHVH, is the greatness, and the power, and the glory, and the victory, and the majesty; for all that is in the heavens and in the earth is yours; yours is the kingdom, YHVH, and you are exalted as head above all" (I Chron. 29:11). "You are YHVH; you alone (Neh. 9:6). "For God alone my soul waits in silence" (Ps. 62:1,5). "You have done great things, O God, who is like you?" (Ps. 71:19). "Blessed be YHVH, the God of Israel, who alone does wondrous things" (Ps. 72:18). "Whom have I in heaven but you? And there is nothing upon earth I desire beside you" (Ps. 73:25). "What god is great like our God?" (Ps. 77:13). "You alone, whose name is YHVH, are the Most High over all the earth" (Ps. 83:18). "You alone are God" (Ps. 86:10). "For who in the skies can be compared to YHVH? Who among the heavenly beings is like YHVH?" (Ps. 89:6–8). "Know that YHVH is God! It is he that made us" (Ps. 100:3). "Who is like YHVH our God?" (Ps. 113:5). "Our Lord is greater than all gods" (Ps. 135:5). "O give thanks to the God of gods…the Lord of lords" (Ps. 136:2–4). "Let them praise the name of YHVH for his name alone is exalted" (Ps. 148:13). "YHVH alone will be exalted in that day" (Isa. 2:11,17). "You are the God, you alone" (Isa. 37:16). "To whom then will you liken God, or what likeness compare with him?" (Isa. 40:18,25). "…before me no god was formed, nor shall there be any after me" (Isa. 43:10). "I am YHVH who made all things. Who was with me?" (Isa. 44:24). "I am YHVH and there is no other. Beside me there is no God" (Isa. 45:5,6,14,18,21,22; 44:6,8; 46:9). "I am the first and I am the last" (Isa. 48:12; 41:4).

"From of old no one has heard or perceived by the ear, no eye has seen a God besides you" (Isa. 64:4). "There is none like you" (Jer. 10:6). "YHVH is the true God; he is the living God and the everlasting King" (Jer. 10:10). "I YHVH am your God and there is none else" (Joel 2:27). "You know no God but me" (Hos. 13:4). "In that day shall YHVH be one, and his name one" (Zech. 14:9). "Have we not all one Father? Has not one God made us?" (Mal. 2:10).

TRINITY IS POLYTHEISM

Despite Scripture's overwhelming testimony to God's absolute unity, incomparableness and exclusiveness, the Trinity persists in Christianity. Although trinitarians insist there are three *persons* in the "godhead" rather than three *gods*, the fact remains that both Jesus and the holy spirit are each considered god—a compromise of God's exclusiveness. In essence, Christians worship a *multiple* deity.

In the Christian Scriptures, virtually every prerogative of God is shared with Jesus, placing him in idolatrous competition with God, in violation of the first two commandments This is what sets Judaism apart from Christianity. Whereas Jews share with Christians the belief in a messiah, they differ as to his nature. The Jewish messiah is a man, not a god (Num. 23:19). He is God's agent and subordinate. For Jews, ascribing the attributes of God to a human is idolatry: "My glory I give to no other, nor my praise to graven images" (Isa. 42:8).

The following comparison-study will demonstrate our thesis:

[CS=Christian Scriptures; HS=Hebrew Scriptures.]

"PRE-HUMAN EXISTENCE" OF JESUS

CS: "In the beginning was the Word, and the Word was with God, and the Word was God...And the Word became flesh" (Jn. 1:1,14).

HS: "I am YHVH who made all things...Who was with me?" (Isa. 44:24). "...before me no god was formed, nor shall there be any after me" (Isa. 43:10). "Whom have I in heaven but you?" (Ps. 73:25).[John says Jesus was with God in the beginning as his co-equal. Isaiah contradicts this and says God had no "co-equal" associate but was the sole Being and Creator!]

JESUS THE IMAGE OF GOD

CS: "He that has seen me has seen the Father" (Jn. 14:9; 12:45). "Christ, who is the image of God" (II Cor. 4:4; Php. 2:6; Col. 1:15,19; 2:9; Heb. 1:3).

HS: "Who among the heavenly beings is like YHVH?" (Ps. 89:6; Exod. 15:11; I Chron. 17:20; Jer. 10:6; Isa. 40:18,25; 46:9). [Although man is "made in the image of God," this does not imply equality. Jesus, on the other hand, is said to be the express image of God implying co-equality. Hebrew Scripture repudiate this.]

"FIRST AND LAST"

CS: "I [Jesus] am the Alpha and the Omega, the first and the last, the beginning and the end" (Rev. 22:13; 1:17,18; 2:8).

HS: "I am the first and I am the last; beside me there is no god......before me no god was formed nor shall there be any after me" (Isa. 44:6; 43:10; 41:4; 48:12). [There cannot be *two* "firsts" and *two* "lasts." God and Jesus cannot *both* share this distinction!]

PRE-EMINENT

CS: Of Jesus: "All authority in heaven and earth has been given to me" (Mt. 28:18; Jn. 3:31). "He is before all things and by him all things consist...that in everything he might have pre-eminence" (Col. 1:17,18; 2:10. Cf. Eph. 1:20,21) "The kingdom of the world has become the kingdom of our Lord and of his Christ and he will rule forever and ever" (Rev. 11:15). "The kingdom of Christ and of God" (Eph. 5:5; cf. Gal. 1:1; II Thess. 2:16). [Christ is mentioned before God!]

HS: "YHVH will reign forever' (Exod. 15:18; Ps. 10:16; 146:10). "Yours, YHVH, is the greatness and the power and the glory and the victory and the majesty . Yours is the kingdom, YHVH, and you are exalted as head above all" (I Chron. 29:11; Cf. Ps. 22:27,28; 148:13; Isa. 33:22; Jer. 10:10; Zech. 14:9.)

"KING OF KINGS, LORD OF LORDS"

CS: Of Jesus: "The Lamb…is Lord of lords and King of kings" (Rev. 17:14; 19:16).

HS: "YHVH your God is God of gods and Lord of lords" (Deut. 10:17; Ps. 136:2,3. Cf. Exod. 15:18; 5:2[3]; 10:16; 22:28; 29:10; 47:6-8; 84:3; 93:1; 103:19; 146:10; Jer. 10; Zech. 14:9).

WORSHIP

CS: "Those in the boat worshiped [Jesus]…" (Mt. 14:33; 28:17; Jn. 9:38). "That at the name of Jesus every knee should bow" (Php. 2:10,11; I Jn. 3:23). "Let all God's angels worship him [Jesus]" (Heb. 1:6). [Paul is quoting Deut. 32:43 and 97:7, according to the Greek Septuagint, where the object of worship is God.]

HS: "You shall worship no other god, for YHVH, whose name is Jealous, is a jealous God" (Exod. 34:14; 20:3; Deut. 4:24; 5:9; 6:13; Josh. 24:19.) "You shall fear YHVH your God; you shall serve him and cleave to him and by his name you shall swear" (Deut. 10:20). "My King and my God…to thee I pray" (Ps. 5:2). "My glory will I not give to another" (Isa. 42:8).

SAVIOR

CS: "Jesus…the source of eternal salvation" (Heb. 5:9).

HS: "Besides me there is no savior" (Isa. 43:11,3; 12:2; Ps. 106:21; Jer. 14:8; Hos. 13:4; Isa. 49:26; 60:16).

CREATOR

CS: "All things were made through [Jesus]" (Jn. 1:3,10; Col. 1:16,17; Heb. 1:2).

HS: "In the beginning God created the heavens and the earth" (Gen. 1:1; Ps. 33:6,9). "You are YHVH, you alone; you made heaven…the earth and all that is in them" (Neh. 9:6). "I am YHVH who made all things, who stretched out the heavens alone, who spread out the earth—Who was with me?" (Isa. 44:24; 40:12,13; 45:12; 48:13; 51:13 and scores of additional references.)

PLURAL FORM ELOHIM NO PROOF OF TRINITY

Trinitarians claim divine plurality is proved by the use of the plural *Elohim* for God in Genesis 1:1. This argument has no basis. *Elohim* may mean either *God* or *gods*. *Eloha*, the singular form for God, is also used: Deut. 32:15; Ps. 18:32). Isa. 44:6,8 uses *Elohim* and *Eloha* interchangeably.

Elohim is used also of foreign gods: When the Israelites had grown impatient at Moses' delayed descent from the mount, they demanded of Aaron: "Make us a god [*Elohim*] which shall go [*yelchu*—plural] before us…(Exod. 32:1,4). See also Deut. 32:39; Exod. 22:20; Judg. 6:31; 9:27,46; 11:24; 16:23; I Sam. 4:7,8; 5:7; I Ki. 11:5,33; 18:27; II Ki. 19:37.

Plural verbs and adjectives also are used with *Elohim*: Gen. 20:13; 35:7; II Sam. 7:23; Deut. 4:7; Josh. 24:19; Prov. 9:10; Ps. 58:12; Deut. 5:26 [H. 23]; I Sam. 17:26,36; Jer. 10:10; 23:36.

Just as the plural form *elohim* is used for a single pagan god, the plural form *adonim*, "lord," is used in like manner: Neh. 3:5. The plural *adonim* is used also of an earthly master: "And Joseph's master [*adonei-Yosef*, p1.] took him…" (Gen. 39:20). See also Gen. 40:1; Exod. 21:4,6,8; I Sam. 20:38; Judg. 3:25. In Isa. 19:4, we have the plural lord with a singular adjective: "And the Egyptians will I give over into the hand of a cruel lord [*adonim kashe*]. Likewise, *Baalim*, lit., masters," is used of an individual: Exod. 22:10,11,13,14.

Thus, the Trinitarian argument based on the usage of the plural form *Elohim* is invalid.

USE OF PLURAL ELOHIM EXPLAINED

Why is the plural *Elohim* used for the one God? Hebrew was spoken by the polytheistic pagans before Israelite monotheism. The plural form for a god was common in Canaan and Phoenicia. In the Tel-el-Amarna letters, the lunar god Sin is addressed as *ilani sa ilani*, "the gods of the gods. The deified Pharaoh is called *ilania*, "my gods." The Phoenicians called their god *elim*, "gods." The Israelites retained the pagan term for God, while adding the name YHVH to make God exclusive. The plural form, Elohim, is termed by grammarians, *pluralis majestatis*, "majestic plural," or *pluralis amplitudinus*, quantitative plural," suggesting infinite fullness. It was a term of respect, whether for God or an earthly master. To suggest that it implies a plural God betrays ignorance of the Hebrew idiom. No reputable Hebrew scholar would concur with the trinitarian argument based on the grammar of Gen. 1:1.

"LET *US* MAKE MAN"

To prove a multiple deity, trinitarians cite Gen. 1:26, "And God said, 'Let *us* make man.'" That God did not *consult* on the preceding five days of Creation is ignored. Moreover, why restrict the *us* to *two* or *three*?

The use of the plural pronoun has been variously explained:

(1) God uses the "majestic plural" in the manner of monarchs, popes, etc. Saadiah states: "The language of Israel gives a distinguished person license to say, Let us do…'" (Cf. Nu. 22:6; Ezra 4:18; Dan. 2:36). If God were a trinity of three co-equal, co-substantial persons, there would be no need for consultation. All three entities would be omniscient!

"YHVH OUR GOD, YHVH IS ONE"

Trinitarians translate Deut. 6:4 as, "Jehovah our *Gods* is Jehovah a unity." They claim the "one of the *Shema* is compound," making God multiple, a "trinity." To support this compound-one" theory, Gen. 2:24 is cited: "The two shall become one flesh." After God has fashioned the woman from Adam's side, Adam declares: "This, now, is bone of my bones and flesh of my flesh. This one shall be called woman because this one was taken from the man" (v. 23). Scripture continues, "Therefore, a man shall leave his father and his mother and cleave to his wife and they shall become *one flesh*" (v. 24). The meaning is clear: "One flesh" does not mean equal status; Scripture is not feminist. The man was first; the woman was created from him, to be *his helper*. The older cannot be equal to the younger! Whereas at first the man was "one" with his father and mother, symbolically he has now become "one" with his wife. In the Trinity, the "Son is *eternally* begotten."

In formulating the doctrine of the Trinity, the Church fathers were confronted with two contradictory aspects of Jesus. On the one hand, as "god," Jesus must be eternal. On the other hand, Jesus is "begotten" of the Father. Thus, the "second person" of the Trinity is said to be "eternally-begotten." But this is confusion. Since the begetter precedes the begotten, there can be no "co-eternality." The husband and wife function as a procreating unit and, ideally, are one in harmony of purpose. However, they are not equal: one may be older, stronger, wiser, etc. The Christian Scriptures make man the authority-figure: "The husband is the head of the wife" (Eph. 5:23).

Husband and wife are a *compound* unit—all units are compound, having multiple components. The unit *one* may be divided into tenths, hundredths, etc. Even the tiny atom has sub-divisions. God is compound—He is Creator, King, Judge, Law-giver, Father, and Husband to Israel—but never a *son*, for God is eternal. These are *functions* of God, not separate persons. A human being may be a son, father, brother, husband, uncle, etc. But these are not separate persons but functions of the same person. The different titles of God represent different aspects of his nature. Unfortunately, this sometimes causes confusion, the Trinity being an example. But the prophet declares the day is coming when there will be no confusion concerning God: "In that day YHVH shall be one and his name one" (Zech. 14:9).

The trinitarian explanation of Deut. 6:4 (the *Shema*) is at variance with Paul: "Although there may be so-called gods in heaven or on earth—as indeed there are many 'gods' and many 'lords'—yet for us there is one God, the Father…and one Lord, Jesus Christ…" (I Cor. 8:5,6). Paul is contrasting the *many* with the one. It would be ludicrous to construe him as saying, "There are many gods in the world but our God is a compound-one—a multiple of three persons." Moreover, where in Paul's equation is the so-called third trinitarian person, "the holy spirit"? Following the reasoning of trinitarians, that the "one" of the *Shema* (Deut. 6:4) is "compound," a "tri-unity," there would be a total of *six* deities in Paul's theology.

Trinitarians argue that if Moses had wanted to teach that God is an *absolute unity,* he would have used *yachid* instead of *echad. Yachid* almost always means an only child" (Gen. 22:2,12,16; Judg. 11:34; Ps. 25:16; 68:7[6]; Prov. 4:3; Jer. 6:26; Amos 8:10; Zach. 12:10. In Ps. 22:21 and 35:17, it means "my only life," in the sense of imperiled or afflicted; cf. Ps. 25:16). Indeed, if Moses had intended to teach that God is "triune," he could have used the Hebrew word *m'shulash,* "threefold" (Eccl. 4:12). But Scripture does use another word to describe God's absolute oneness: *l'vad,* "alone": "YHVH, the God of Israel…you are he, the God, you *alone* (II Ki. 19:15,19; cf. Neh. 9:6; Ps. 72:18; 148:13; Isa. 2:11,17).

A missionary tract states: "There are scores of passages in the *Tanach* [Hebrew Scriptures] that prove God is a plurality within a unity ['three in one']." We have not found these scores of passages. The tract offers Isa. 42:1: "Behold my servant, whom I uphold, my chosen, in whom my soul delights; I have put my spirit upon him…The tract imagines Trinity in this passage—God, *Messiah, Spirit.* But this desperate attempt betrays ignorance of the Tanach: The servant" is Israel: "Jacob my servant, Israel whom I have chosen" (Isa. 44:1). Both the servant" and the "spirit" are subordinate to God, not "co-equal," as in the Trinity.

The tract quotes Isaiah 61:1: "The spirit of the Lord YHVH is upon me, because YHVH has anointed me…" Again, the tract envisions Trinity. Luke applies this verse to Jesus (Lu. 4:18-21). The one anointed, however, is subordinate to the anointer. No "co-equality"! Moreover, there are *four* mentioned: *Spirit Lord, YHVH,* and the one *anointed!*

The tract cites Prov. 30:4: "Who has ascended to heaven and come down? Who has gathered the wind in his fists? Who has wrapped up the waters in a garment? Who has established all the ends of the earth? What is his name, and what is his son's name? Surely you know!" For trinitarians this suggests "Father and Son" . But this is careless exegesis. The passage is not about a "spiritual" heaven but about the sky, starry heavens, wind, waters and earth. The questions are rhetorical, conveying the inability of finite humans to comprehend the wonders of God's creation. Cf., "Who has measured the waters in the hollow of his hand and marked off the heavens with a span, enclosed the dust of the earth in a measure and weighed the mountains in scales and the hills in a balance?…Who has directed the spirit of YHVH or as his counselor instructed him?…To whom then will you liken God…?" (Isa. 40:12-14,18,25; Job 34:13; 38:4-11.) The above contradicts the trinitarian notion that God was assisted in the creation (Jn. 1:3; Isa. 44:24.) For the expression, "his name…son's name," compare, "God is not man, that he should lie, or a son of man, that he should repent" (Nu. 23:19). "What is man that you are mindful of him, and the son of man that you care for him" (Ps. 8:4). In the above, "man" and "son of man" are synonymous. "What is his son's name?" is meant only to intensify the rhetoric. The passage in Prov. 30 concludes with the caveat: "Do not add to his words lest he reprove you and you be found a liar" (v. 6). Missionaries should heed this and not read spurious trinitarian notions into the text!

MONOTHEISM, KEYSTONE OF ISRAEL'S FAITH

Monotheism, the belief in *one*, exclusive God, is the keystone of Israel's faith and an all-pervasive theme of Hebrew Scripture. Although Trinitarians claim God is one because surely they cannot ignore Scripture's unequivocal declaration of this, the Trinity, in effect, postulates a "second god," co-equal and co-eternal with God the Creator. Using "persons" instead of "gods" in the definition of the Trinity does not alter the fact that the absolute singularity of God has been compromised.

The doctrine of a "triune" god is foreign to Hebrew Scripture. In fact, scholars doubt that it was part of the early Christian belief-system: "The doctrine of the Trinity is not a product of the earliest Christian period and we do not find it carefully expressed before the end of the second century (*God and the One God*, Robert M. Grant, p. 156).

Trinitarians follow the wrong procedure: they *begin* with a doctrine, then try desperately to make Scripture conform to it. Scripture should determine belief, not vice versa. Trinitarians are uneasy about the Trinity and hard-pressed to support it scripturally, for indeed the Hebrew Scriptures are unequivocal about God's exclusive oneness and nowhere mention "Trinity." Trinitarians acknowledge the contradiction of a supposed incarnate deity who exhibits human traits; who prays to *God*; who says, "My father is greater than I"; who declares he came not to do his own will but the will of him who sent him; who at the end questions why God has forsaken him; who suffers and dies. They find it difficult to reconcile the statement, "No man has ever seen God," with Jesus' claim, "He that has seen me has seen the Father." The "god-man" theory, that Jesus was both human and divine does not help. Nor are we helped by the explanation that the "mystery" of the Trinity cannot be understood by human logic but must be accepted on faith. The Trinity is a teaching of confusion (I Cor. 14:33).

Trinitarians take a cue from Paul, who himself was defensive about his teachings: "We impart a sacred and *hidden wisdom* of God—in words not taught by human wisdom but taught by the spirit" (I Cor. 2:7,13). Paul spoke of "the mystery hidden for ages but now made manifest" (Col. 1:26; Eph. 3:9). For Jews, however, that GOD IS ONE, is no "hidden mystery" (cf. Isa. 48:16; Deut. 30:11-14; 29:29).

THE TRINITY AND "MESSIANIC JUDAISM"

The name "Yeshua-Jesus" is constantly on the lips of "Messianic Jews," who offer prayer in his name. One wonders whom "Messianic Jews" are thinking of when they say "Lord"? Jesus said, "No one can serve two masters" (Mt. 6:24). "You shall worship the Lord your God and *him only* shall you serve" (Mt. 4:10). Did Jesus include *himself* in this worship?

"Messianic Jews" studiously avoid the name "Christian." What they are saying is, that "Christians" have departed from the "pristine" teachings of "Yeshua-Messiah," whereas "Messianic Jews" have restored the "pure" and "original" faith. We have observed this phenomenon in other religious groups who, when seeking uniqueness and originality, distance themselves from the "orthodox" believers, claiming that they, the new believers, are the "authentic" ones.

It is astonishing to us, therefore, that the "Messianic" movement clings to the Trinity, which they have renamed "Tri-unity." Despite their vehement criticism that the Catholic Church has introduced "pagan" doctrines, the "Messianic" movement still adheres to the Trinity, a word coined by Tertullian, a Church father, and accepted into Church cannon-law at the Council of Nicea in 325. In perpetuating this doctrine of the "tri-une" nature of God, the "Messianic" movement forfeits its right to be called "Jewish," for a Jew cannot believe that "God is three."

"Messianic Jews" challenge the accuracy of the name "Jesus," claiming that the Greek *Iesous* is not his authentic name but that he was called *Yeshua*, or *Yehoshua*. They trust that eventually ancient documents will come to light to prove their claim. Rather then focusing on this question, however, "Messianic Jews" would do better to concern themselves with the *nature* of God as revealed in Hebrew Scripture—that is, if they are serious about their claim to be "Jewish."

MONOTHEISM VS. POLYTHEISM

The issue addressed in this chapter, namely the PERCEPTION of God, is of no little consequence. Essentially, the issue is MONOTHEISM vs. POLYTHE-ISM—whether God is singular or plural.

This was a matter of crucial importance for ancient Israel. When the Israelites fashioned a golden calf at Sinai, proclaiming it "God," their sin was so great God would have destroyed them had not Moses intervened (Exod. 32). Who cannot read the fourth chapter of Deuteronomy and not be moved by the seriousness of its warning against idolatry and its dire consequences:

"YHVH spoke to you out of the midst of the fire; you heard the voice of words but saw no form…Take good heed to yourselves, therefore, for you saw no manner of form on the day YHVH spoke to you in Horeb out of the midst of the fire—lest you deal corruptly and make yourselves a graven image, even the form of any figure, the likeness of male or female…and lest you lift up your eyes to the heavens and when you see the sun and the moon and the stars, even all the host of heaven, you be drawn away and worship them, and serve them…for YHVH your God is a devouring fire, a jealous God…Know this day, and lay it to heart, that YHVH, He is God in heaven above and upon the earth beneath; there is none else" (Deut. 4:12, 15–19,24,35,39). If God is "jealous" of *graven* images, how much more so of a deified human!

The deification of Jesus compromises God's uniqueness and incomparability: Jesus shares God's glory; is in the "form of God"; is the "first and the last"; is the creator; is pre-eminent; is worshiped as god!

The Christian doctrine of the Trinity contradicts God's own declaration of his UNITY in the *Shema*: "Hear, O Israel, YHVH our God, YHVH is ONE" (Deut. 6:4). The *Shema* was vouchsafed to the Jewish People. For upwards of three-thousand years, they have safeguarded this most important teaching, namely, that God is exclusively and uncompromisingly ONE. The Jews have never understood the ONE of the *Shema* to mean anything other than ONE. Indeed, in the ancient Masoretic text, *Echad* (Heb. "one") is written with an enlarged *daled* to avoid the error of pronouncing it *acher*, "other."

"ADDING" TO GOD'S WORD

The Trinity, or "Tri-unity," is a blatant example of "adding to God's Word" (Deut. 4:2), and a clear violation of the commandment, "You shall have no other gods before me" (Exod. 20:3). It is nothing more than disguised polytheism. "Messianic Jews" who embrace this doctrine belie their claim to be "Jewish."

CHAPTER 3

"GOD IS NOT A MAN"

"GOD HAS COME DOWN TO EARTH"

One of the cardinal doctrines of Christianity is the "Incarnation": "Jesus Christ, our Redeemer, is the Son of God made man; hence He is God himself…The heathen had very early conceived the idea that God had descended from heaven and mixed with men; the Greek mythology is full of it. Now God has actually come down to earth" (*The Catechism Explained*, Francis Spirago, Richard F. Clarke [ed.], 1899). "The Incarnation of the Son of God is a mystery which we cannot understand, but only admire and honor…I know that the Son of God became man, but how I do not know" (St. John Chrysostom, ibid.).

The following are the Christian Scripture proof-texts for Incarnation: "In the beginning was the word and the word was with God and the word was God. And the word became flesh and dwelt among us…" (Jn. 1:1,14,18; 3:13,31; 6:33,50,51,58; 8:23,58; 10:38; 16:28; 17:5,24; Heb. 2:14;). [The "Word" is Jesus; the event "Incarnation"—"God assuming flesh."] "Philip said to him, 'Lord, show us the Father, and we shall be satisfied.' Jesus said to him…'He who has seen me has seen the Father'" (Jn. 14:8–11; 12:45). "Who being in the form of God, did not count equality with God a thing to be grasped, but emptied himself, taking the form of a servant, being born in the likeness of men" (Php. 2:6,7). "He is the image of the invisible God…For in him, the whole fullness of deity dwells bodily" (Col. 1:15,19; 2:9). "He reflects the glory of God and bears the very stamp of his nature" (Heb. 1:3).

The following however, seem to contradict Incarnation: Paul had healed a cripple and the crowds paid homage to him, saying: "The gods have come down to us in the likeness of men." Paul admonishes them: "Men, why are you doing this? We also are men…turn from these vain things to a living God who made the heaven and the earth and the sea and all that is in them" (Acts 14:8–15). Where in Paul's words is there any room for Incarnation?

"UP, MAKE US A GOD!"

The pagan idea of apprehending God with the physical senses—"image-worship"—is alluded to early in Scripture. At the burning bush, when God tells Moses He will free the Hebrew slaves, Moses doubts that the Israelites will believe him. He anticipates how difficult it will be for the Israelites, who had been idol-worshipers, to worship an unseen God (Exod. ch. 3). Indeed, this difficulty was dramatically manifested at Sinai when the Israelites, impatient at Moses return from Sinai, demanded of Aaron: "Up, make us a god, who shall go before us" (Exod. 32:1). Their sin of idolatry is recalled in the Psalms: "They made a calf in Horeb, and worshiped a molten image. They exchanged the glory of God for the image of a grass-eating ox. They forgot God their Savior who had done great things in Egypt" (Ps. 106:19–21; cf. I Ki. 12:28). Paul characterizes idolatry similarly: "[They] exchanged the glory of the Immortal God for images resembling mortal man or birds or animals or reptiles…they exchanged the truth about God for a lie and worshiped and served the creature more than the Creator" (Rom. 1:23,25; cf. Jn. 4:24). Paul's censure of idolatry seems a fitting repudiation of the Christian doctrine of Incarnation. The "truth about God" is that he is Infinite— a Spirit-being. To say "God became flesh" is to deny the essential nature of God! God cannot be represented in finite form. To worship a man as God, according to Paul, is to "worship and serve the creature more than the Creator." The prophet Jeremiah warns: "Cursed is the man who trusts in man and makes *flesh* his arm"…(Jer. 17:5–7; 146:3,4). Samuel said, "The Glory of Israel will not lie or repent; for *He is not a man*" (I Sam. 15:29; cf. Num. 23:19; Hos. 11:9). The Creator cannot be confined in created matter! This is the essence of Hebrew Monotheism, as proclaimed throughout Hebrew Scripture.

THE INFINITE GOD NOT CONFINABLE IN MATTER

To attempt to depict God is to limit the Unlimited One, to *define* (make finite) the Infinite One. God is omnipresent; "Where shall I go from Your spirit? Or where shall I flee from Your presence? If I ascend to heaven, You are there! If I make my bed in Sheol, You are there! If I take the wings of the morning and dwell in the uttermost parts of the sea, even there shall Your hand lead me, and Your right hand hold me…" (Ps. 139:7–12; cf. Isa. 66:1). The Incarnation would confine God in a human body, in denial of His *universal* presence. Since God is everywhere, there is no need for him to assume physical form in order to manifest Himself. God is at once transcendent and immanent. Maimonides held: "One who conceives God corporeally is an apostate" (*Mishneh Torah, T'shuvah* III, 7). He said: "If I could describe God, he would not be God" (*Guide*, I Ch. 59, p. 88b).

The desire to apprehend God with the physical senses stems from an immature religious personality which cannot relate to an abstract God but must visualize God in a familiar form. God need not materialize flesh to be accessible; He is ever available to those who sincerely call upon Him: "YHVH is near to all who call upon him, to all who call upon him in truth" (Ps. 145:18). "I dwell in the high and holy place and also with him who is of a contrite and humble spirit" (Isa. 57:15). "For what great nation is there that has a god so near to it as YHVH our God is to us, whenever we call upon him?" (Deut. 4:7). "You, YHVH, are in the midst of us…(Jer. 14:9; cf. Exod. 25:8; 29:45; Lev. 26:11,12; Num. 5:3; I Ki. 6:13; Ezek. 43:9; Zech. 2:10,11 [Heb. 14,15]; 8:3). "Am I a God at hand, says YHVH, and not a God afar off? Can a man hide himself in secret places so that I cannot see him? says YHVH. Do I not fill heaven and earth? says YHVH" (Jer. 23:23,24). God cannot be contained in an earthly structure or, by extension, in a human body: "But will God indeed dwell on the earth? Behold, the heaven and heaven of heavens cannot contain You; how much less this house which I have built!" (I Ki. 8:27). God's domain is in the heavens—the *spirit* world. It contradicts His nature to assume a physical form: "The heavens, even the heavens, are YHVH's; but the earth has He given to the children of man" (Ps. 115:16).

There is no need for God to appear as an earthling; His dominion *includes* the earth: He is "God in heaven above and on earth beneath" (Josh. 2:11). "The whole earth is filled with His glory" (Isa. 6:3).

"YOU CANNOT SEE MY FACE"

There has always been a deep, psychological need to *see* the deity. Indeed, Moses himself asked God: "I pray You, show me Your glory." God replied, "I will make all My *goodness* pass before you, and will proclaim before you my name 'YHVH'; .But *you cannot see my face*; for man shall not see me and live." And YHVH said, "Behold, there is a place by me where you shall stand upon the rock; and while my glory passes by I will put you in a cleft of the rock, and I will cover you with my hand until I have passed by; then I will take away my hand, and you shall see my back; but my face shall not be seen" (Exod. 33:18–23). Moses asked to see God's *glory*, not his actual being. God's "goodness" would pass before Moses but Moses would not see God's "face"! Here we have the essence of spiritual religion. A true encounter with God is to apprehend his "goodness"—his attributes of justice, mercy and lovingkindness (Mic. 6:8).

But what of the instances where God spoke to Moses "face to face"? "When Moses entered the tent, the pillar of cloud would descend and stand at the door of the tent, and YHVH would speak with Moses...*face to face, as a man speaks to his friend*" (Exod. 33:9–11). "With him [Moses] I speak *mouth to mouth*...and he *beholds the form* of YHVH..." (Num. 12:8). "And there has not arisen a prophet since in Israel like Moses, whom YHVH knew *face to face*" (Deut. 34:10). In one place we have, "You cannot see my face"; but here..."YHVH knew [Moses] *face to* face."! Moses said to Israel: "YHVH spoke with you face to face at the mount out of the midst of the fire" (Deut. 5:4). If God spoke to them "out of the midst of the fire," surely they did not behold him. When Moses sought reassurance that God would be with him, God told him: "My presence [*panai*, lit. my face'] will go with you" ['I will *personally* accompany you'] (Exod. 33:14). The expression "face to face," then, may be understood as an intimate, personal encounter, without a mediator.

We find Num. 12:6-8 very instructive: "If there be a prophet among you, I shall make YHVH known to him in the vision; I shall speak to him in the dream. Not so my servant Moses; he is faithful in all my house. I shall speak with him mouth to mouth, clearly, and not in dark speeches; and the likeness of YHVH shall he behold..." We must contrast the above with God's declaration to Moses, "my face shall not be seen" (Exod. 33:18–23). We also recall God's warning to Moses: "Go down, warn the people not to break through to YHVH to gaze and many of them fall" (Exod. 20:21-23). Thus we have two traditions regarding Moses' experience with God: In one, Moses is not permitted to observe the form of God; in the other he does behold God. With the prophets, however, God communicates only through visions and dreams. *The general populace, however, may not view God!*

TWO TRADITIONS

Scripture is not a monolithic document. Two traditions are at work here. Exod. 33:18–20 ("you cannot see my face") is assigned by scholars to *J* (the *Jahwistic* document); vv. 9—11, "YHVH used to speak with Moses face to face," is assigned to *E* (the *Elohistic* document).

Another example of the fusion of two, apparently diverse, traditions is Exodus, chapter 24: "And he said to Moses, 'Come up to YHVH, you and Aaron, Nadab, and Abihu, and seventy of the elders of Israel, and worship afar off. Moses alone shall approach YHVH; but the others shall not come near, and the people shall not come up with him...Then Moses and Aaron, Nadab, and Abihu, and seventy of the elders of Israel went up, and they saw the God of Israel; and there was under his feet as it were a pavement of sapphire stone, like the very heaven for clearness. And he did not lay his hand on the chief men of the people Israel; they saw a vision of [*va-ye-che-zu*] God, and ate and drank...Then Moses went up on the mountain, and the cloud covered the mountain. The glory of YHVH settled on Mount Sinai, and the cloud covered it six days; and on the seventh day he called to Moses out of the midst of the cloud. Now the appearance of the glory of YHVH was like a devouring fire on the top of the mountain in the sight of the people of Israel..." (Exod. 24:1,2,9–11,15–17).

First they are told to "worship afar off"; "Moses alone shall approach YHVH. Then we are told: "They *saw* the God of Israel...they *saw a vision of God*..." God is not described in human terms: The appearance of YHVH was like a *devouring fire*..." God is hidden, as it were: God calls to Moses "out of the *midst of the cloud.*" Only a glorious emanation is perceived, symbolized by the blue sapphire, heaven-like expanse. God is hidden by clouds and fire. He is ineffable. This constitutes the *second* time Moses ascends the mountain. Compare the first ascent: "And YHVH said to Moses, 'Lo, I am coming to you in a thick cloud...And the people stood afar off while Moses drew near to the thick darkness where God was. And YHVH said to Moses, 'Thus shall you say to the people of Israel: "You have seen for yourselves that I have talked with you *from heaven*. You shall not make gods of silver to be with me, nor shall you make for yourselves gods of gold" (Exod. 19:9; 20:21,22): Because they saw no image—God spoke to them from heaven—they were warned against making an image of God: "YHVH spoke to you out of the midst of the fire; you heard the sound of words, *but saw no form*; there was only a voice...Therefore take good heed to yourselves. Since *you saw no form* on the day YHVH spoke to you at Horeb out of the midst of the fire, beware lest you act corruptly by making a graven image for yourselves, in the form of any figure, the likeness of male or female" (Deut. 4:12-16).

The prophet Ezekiel has an encounter reminiscent of the Sinai experience: "The heavens were opened, and I saw *visions of God*...seated above the likeness of a throne was a likeness, as it were, of a human form Such was the appearance of the likeness of the glory of YHVH" (Ezek. 1:26). What Ezekiel experienced was a dream-vision, not an actual sighting. Cf. Gen. 46:2; Num. 12:6; 24:3,4; Job 4:13; Dan. 1:17; 2:19, 28; 4:5.

The vision of Micaiah is explained similarly: "I saw YHVH sitting on his throne, and all the hosts of heaven standing by him on his right hand and on his left" (I Ki. 22:19). Again, this is a dream-vision, as suggested by verse 17.

In the above accounts, the "form" of God is never described. Only in special places does Moses have encounters with God—on top of the mount, "in a place by me," or, in the "Tent of Meeting." God appears in a "pillar of cloud," obscured from the people. Incarnation—God assuming flesh-and-blood—violates God's warning to Israel against making "any figure, the likeness of male or female." Nevertheless, we do observe *two traditions* woven in and through Scripture—a kind of theological process refining and resolving the relationship of man and God. We see the ancient pagan notion of encountering a physical image of God giving way to God as spirit, immaterial, present with man although not visually seen. For us, then, the Christian doctrine of Incarnation—God becoming man— is a regression to paganism.

"TO WHOM WILL YOU COMPARE ME?"

Even staunch monotheists, who argue passionately that God is spirit, may yield to the tendency to envision God as a super-human. But "God is spirit" (Jn. 4:24); there can be no humanity in heaven (Rom. 1:23; I Co. 15:40–50). The infinite God is inscrutable: "Can you find out the deep things of God? Can you find out the limit of the Almighty? It is higher than heaven—what can you do?" (Job 11:7-9; see also 26:14; Eccl. 3:11). "You are a God who hides yourself..." (Isa. 45:15,16). "To whom then will you compare me, that I should be like him? says the Holy One...his understanding is unsearchable" (Isa. 40:25,28). "His greatness is unsearchable" (Ps. 145:3). God is not to be depicted.

"I HAVE SET YHVH ALWAYS BEFORE ME"

Christians speak of a "*personal* Savior," with whom they claim to have an intimate relationship. Biblical man already enjoyed a "personal relationship" with the *invisible* God. David's God was caring and provident: "YHVH is my shepherd, I shall not want...I have set YHVH always before me. Because He is at my right hand, I shall never be moved" (Ps. 23:1; 16:8;). Biblical man "walked with God" (Gen. 5:22; 6:9; 17:1; 24:40; 48:15; Mic. 6:8) and felt the presence of God (Gen. 16:13; 28:15,16; 46:4).

God need not materialize to make Himself accessible to man. The notion that "seeing is believing" is pagan and juvenile. Even Paul affirms that "we walk by faith"; that "faith is the evidence of things not seen" (II Cor. 5:7; Heb. 11:1; Cf. Rom. 8:24,25; II Cor. 4:18). For the mature religious personality, the heavenly, spiritual Deity is sufficient: "Whom have I in heaven but you? And there is nothing upon earth that I desire besides you" (Ps. 73:25).

So pervasive was Hebrew Monotheism that none of the ancient Biblical heroes was venerated. To prevent the deification of Moses, his burial place was kept forever secret (Deut. 34:6).

"NO MAN HAS SEEN GOD"

The Christian Scriptures are not of one voice regarding Incarnation. The following passages contradict Incarnation:

"No man has seen God at any time" (Jn. 1:18; 1 Jn. 4:12). "God is spirit" (Jn. 4:24). "His voice you have never heard, his form you have never seen (Jn. 5:37). "[God] alone has immortality, dwelling in the light which no man can approach unto; whom no man has seen or can see (I Tim. 6:16). "For us there is *one God*...and one Lord Jesus Christ" (I Cor. 8:6; cf. Eph. 4:5, 6; I Tim. 2:5). "And this is eternal life, that they might know you, the *only* true God, and Jesus Christ whom you have sent" (Jn. 17:3). Jesus said, "I ascend to my God and your God" (Jn. 20:17). The above statements would be illogical if Jesus were God.

"YHVH WAS NOT IN THE WIND"

The mature religious personality has no need to imagine God in a tangible form. God relates spiritually, not physically, to man. God instructed Elijah the prophet: "Go forth, and stand upon the mount before YHVH. And behold, YHVH passed by, and a great and strong wind rent the mountains, and broke in pieces the rocks before YHVH, but YHVH was not in the wind; and after the wind an earthquake, but YHVH was not in the earthquake; and after the earthquake a fire, but YHVH was not in the fire; and after the fire a still small voice" (I Ki. 19:9–12; cf. Job 9:11). God need not appear physically to us. He speaks to our hearts—in the "still small voice."

Christianity sees the Incarnation as an expression of God's love: God *personally* descends to earth to dwell among us and retrieve us from sin (Jn. 3:16; Rom. 8:3). But this only reinforces man's helplessness! Greater love is to require that man *himself* be responsible for overcoming sin (Gen. 4:7).

INCARNATION A REGRESSION TO PAGANISM

Because Incarnation is unsupportable by Scripture and defies logic, Christian theologians call it a "mystery." Paul censures those who believe the gods descended bodily to the earth: "Because they exchanged the truth about God for a lie and worshiped and served the creature more than the creator" (Rom. 1:25). The *infinite* God is not confinable to matter. He need not be present physically: "His glory fills the whole earth" (Isa. 6:3; Jer. 23:23,24). Although Scripture says Moses glimpsed God, the people at large were never so privileged. Indeed, Moses was told, "You cannot see my face." As for the Israelites, "They heard the sound but saw *no form*" (Deut. 4:12).

When angels appeared, they had no identity apart from God. Their appearances were temporary. No cult was dedicated to their worship. The wish to "see God" is religious immaturity. The mature religious personality is content with God's *invisible* presence.

Incarnation is a denial of the Creator's immortal nature. It is a regression to paganism.

CHAPTER 4

"GOD OF VENGEANCE/GOD OF LOVE" FALLACY

The "God of the Hebrew Scriptures" has been characterized as a "God of vengeance," as contrasted with the "God of the Christian Scriptures" who is portrayed as a "God of love." We believe this characterization to be an anti-Jewish bias that is patently one-sided and unscholarly, emphasizing certain passages to the exclusion of others.

Indeed, the Christian Scriptures do speak of a God of love: "God so loved the world that he gave his only begotten son" (Jn. 3:16; I Jn. 4:8,9). For us, however, God's alleged sacrifice of his son for the world's sins does not exemplify love. If, for example, a child were to damage a neighbor's property and the parents made restitution, it would not necessarily show love. We believe greater love and wisdom would require the *child* to pay for the damages out of earned income or repair the damages himself. This would be a learning experience for the child.

God's loving scheme for man is not vicarious atonement but obedience to law: "Obedience is better than sacrifice" (I Sam. 15:22). "To do righteousness and justice is more acceptable to the LORD than sacrifice" (Prov. 21:3; Hos. 6:6). God demonstrates his faith in man by encouraging him to overcome sinfulness through the discipline of law (Gen. 4:7; Ps. 119:33,92,93).

A "NEW COMMANDMENT"—"LOVE ONE ANOTHER"

Jesus said: "You have heard it was said, 'You shall love your neighbor and hate your enemies.' But I say to you, Love your enemies" (Mt. 5:43,44). "A new commandment I give you, that you love one another" (Jn. 13:34). But this commandment is not new! Moses already taught: "You shall love your neighbor as yourself" (Lev. 19:18). There *is* no commandment to "hate your enemies." Although Israel was not commanded to love one's enemy, an enemy was to be treated with justice and mercy: "If you meet your enemy's ox or his ass going astray, you shall surely return it to him" (Exod. 23:4,5). "If your enemy is hungry, give him bread to eat; and if he is thirsty, give him water to drink" (Prov. 25:21).

Jesus said, "If any one strikes you on the right cheek, turn to him the other also" (Mt. 5:39). But Jesus did not lovingly "turn the other cheek" when he drove out the money-changers from the temple (Mt. 21:12); or when he said to the Pharisees, "You are of your father the devil" (Jn. 8:44)! Neither did Paul follow his master's teaching when, having been struck on the mouth, he railed back, "God strike you, you whitewashed wall!" (Acts 23:2,3). Jesus taught, "Bless them that curse you" (Luke 6:28). But contrast Paul's vindictiveness: "Alexander the coppersmith did me great harm; the Lord requite him for his deeds!" (II Tim. 4:14). "If we or an angel from heaven preach to you a gospel contrary to that which we have preached to you, let him be accursed" (Gal. 1:8). Concerning the "unruly" tongue, James taught: "With it we bless the Lord and Father, and with it we curse men, who are made in the likeness of God" (James 3:9). Contrast James' admonition with Paul's salutation to the Corinthians: "If any one has no love for the Lord, let him be accursed…My love be with you all in Christ Jesus. Amen" (I Cor. 16:21–24). With one breath Paul calls down a curse upon unbelievers and with the second he blesses his brethren!

THE "GOD OF THE CHRISTIAN SCRIPTURES" NOT ALWAYS LOVING

The God of the Christian Scriptures" is not always *loving*: "It is a fearful thing to fall into the hands of the living God!" (Heb. 10:31). "Our God is a consuming fire" (Heb. 12:29). "The wrath of God is revealed from heaven against all ungodliness and wickedness of men" (Rom. 1:18). "…when the Lord Jesus is revealed from heaven with his mighty angels in flaming fire, inflicting *vengeance* upon those who do not know God and upon those who do not obey the gospel of our Lord Jesus. They shall suffer the punishment of eternal destruction and exclusion from the presence of our Lord" (II Thess. 1:7,8). "He that believes not the Son shall not see life, but the wrath of God abides upon him" (Jn. 3:36).

GOD OF LOVE IN THE HEBREW SCRIPTURES

The Hebrew Scriptures speak of a God of love as well as a God of justice: YHVH, YHVH, a God merciful and gracious, slow to anger, and abounding in steadfast love and faithfulness…" (Exod. 34:6; Ps. 86:5,15). "Who is a God like You, pardoning iniquity and passing over transgression for the remnant of his inheritance? He does not retain his anger forever because he delights in steadfast love" (Mic. 7:18). "Righteousness and justice are the foundation of Your throne; steadfast love and faithfulness go before You" (Ps. 89:14). "…I am YHVH who practices steadfast love, justice, and righteousness in the earth" (Jer. 9:24).

If we are to speak of a "God of vengeance," what could be crueler than the notion that God would damn millions because they did not accept the "Christian" way of salvation!

God stands for justice *and* mercy. It is wrong to characterize him as being for one or the other.

CHAPTER 5

JESUS

The name "Jesus" is from the Greek *Iesous*, which translates the Hebrew *Yehoshua*, "saved of Yah." "Messianic Jews" refer to Jesus as *Yeshua* and often explain it as meaning "salvation," implying that Jesus himself was salvation." *Yeshua*, however, does not mean "salvation." Salvation in Hebrew is *Yeshuah*, a similar word ending in *heh*. A number of Israelites bore the name *Yeshua* (I Chron. 24:11; II Chron. 31:15; Ezra ch. 2) and it was a common name in the first century. Josephus mentions nineteen individuals so named. In modern Hebrew Jesus is *Yeshu*.

Why do "Messianic Jews" insist on using "Yeshua" rather than Jesus? They contend that when Jesus revealed himself to Saul on the road to Damascus, Jesus spoke Hebrew (Acts 9). If this is the case, it is more likely Jesus used *Yehoshua*, not *Yeshua*. Another reason why they use the Hebrew name is to create an appearance of "Jewishness," thus distancing themselves from mainstream Christianity and making themselves more acceptable to potential Jewish converts. By the same token, Jews will continue to use the Greek form to avoid the appearance that we acknowledge the so-called "Jewishness" of "Messianic Judaism"—for we do not. The religion of Jesus was fairly cleansed of its Jewish elements, with the introduction of pagan teachings, such as Virgin-birth, Incarnation, Trinity, and human sacrifice.

BIRTH OF JESUS

The following is Luke's account of the birth of Jesus: "In the sixth month the angel Gabriel was sent from God to a city of Galilee named Nazareth, to a virgin betrothed to a man whose name was Joseph, of the house of David; and the virgin's name was Mary...And the angel said to her...'you will conceive in your womb and bear a son, and you shall call his name Jesus. He will be great, and will be called the Son of the Most High; and the Lord God will give him the throne of his father David, and he will reign over the house of Jacob forever; and of his kingdom there will be no end.' And Mary said to the angel, 'How can this be, since I have no husband?' And the angel said to her, 'The Holy Spirit will come upon you, and the power of the Most High will overshadow you; therefore the child to be born will be called holy, the son of God'" (Lu. 1:26–35). Luke subsequently traces Jesus lineage through Joseph, to King David, to Adam (Lu. 3: 23–38).

Matthew records: "When his mother Mary had been betrothed to Joseph, before they came together, she was found to be with child of the Holy Spirit; and her husband Joseph, being a just man and unwilling to put her to shame, resolved to divorce her quietly. But as he considered this, behold, an angel of the Lord appeared to him in a dream, saying, 'Joseph, son of David, do not fear to take Mary your wife, for that which is conceived in her is of the Holy Spirit; she will bear a son, and you shall call his name Jesus, for he will save his people from their sins.' All this took place to fulfill what the Lord has spoken by the prophet: 'Behold, a virgin shall conceive and bear a son, and his name shall be called Emmanuel (which means, God with us). When Joseph awoke from sleep, he did as the angel of the Lord commanded him; he took his wife, but knew her not until she had borne a son; and he called his name Jesus" (Mt. 1:18–25). Matthew traces Jesus' lineage through Joseph, to David, to Abraham.

ANALYSIS OF THE TWO BIRTH ACCOUNTS

In Luke the angel appears to Mary in Nazareth. In Matthew he appears to Joseph, without mention of the city. The question of divorce is mentioned only in Matthew. In Luke Mary names the child. In Matthew Joseph names him. In Luke Jesus is to rule upon the throne of David over the house of Jacob forever. Matthew omits this.

"TRINITY" ABSENT IN THE BIRTH ACCOUNTS

In Christian theology, Jesus is "God the son," second person of the Trinity. In a crucial location, at the beginning of the Gospels of Luke and Matthew, where the birth of Jesus is announced, the trinitarian concept is absent and in fact is contradicted: The child Jesus "will be great," not "greatest." The *Lord God* gives him the throne, implying that the child is not "God." If it is argued that it refers to the "human" Jesus, note that "he rules forever and his kingdom is eternal." He is called, not "God the son," but "son of the Most high." As such, he cannot be *co-equal* with "God the Father"!

A VIRGIN SHALL CONCEIVE"

According to Matthew, Jesus' birth "took place to fulfill what the Lord had spoken by the prophet: 'Behold, a virgin shall conceive and bear a son, and his name shall be called Emmanuel, which means, God with us'" (Mt. 1:22,23; Isa. 7:14). The question of the Virgin Birth is crucial, for on it depends the whole doctrine of Christian Salvation. According to Christian theology, when Adam sinned, he forfeited immortality for all his descendants. To atone for Adam's sin, a perfect life had to be sacrificed (Jn. 3:16; Mt. 20:28). Since all of Adam's descendants were tainted with his "original sin," ordinary humans could not produce a sinless offspring. Miraculously, a heavenly life form—the second person of the Trinity—was transferred to the womb of the virgin Mary. Thus, Jesus was born without male intervention, producing a "god-man" (Jn. 1:1,14; I Cor. 15:45)...Thus, the Christian doctrine of atonement.

In the birth-accounts of Matthew and Luke, there is no direct statement that a "heavenly life" was implanted in Mary's womb. The record says only: "That which is conceived in her is of Holy Spirit" (Mt. 1:20). (The Greek lacks the definite article.) There is no mention of any so-called pre-human existence of Jesus or of his alleged divinity. We find it interesting that of John the Baptist it is said: "...he will be filled with the Holy Spirit, even from his mother's womb" (Lu. 1:15). The "virgin-birth" is known only to Matthew and Luke and is not mentioned by Mark or John, or for that matter, by Paul (cf. Gal. 4:4).

Jesus had to be man for two reasons: 1. To be Adam's equal; 2. To be David's descendant. But as Adam's descendant, how could Jesus be sinless? The Protestant theologian John Calvin (1509-61) claimed Jesus was "sanctified by the Holy Spirit." The Catholic Church in 1854 declared Mary was conceived without original sin—"The Immaculate Conception." Being sinless, she would not transmit sin to her offspring.

In a tract by a radio evangelist (a medical doctor), the following was advanced: "Mary provided the body of Jesus and the Holy Spirit provided the life and blood. Sin is in the blood, not the flesh. The blood of Jesus, therefore, was sinless. While the mother contributes all the necessary elements for the developing embryo, no actual blood-tissue passes from mother to embryo." ("The Virgin Birth of Jesus"—M. R. DeHaan, M.D., Grand Rapids, Michigan.)

The above tract, written during the Hitler era, was subsequently refuted by a publication of the American Board of Missions to the Jews, which maintained that the doctor-evangelist, by denying Jesus had Jewish blood, was unwittingly espousing the Nazi Aryan-race theory.

The evangelist-doctor evidently had overlooked Mt. 26:41; Mk. 14:38; Rom. 7:18; 8:3; Gal. 5:24; I Jn. 2:16, all of which affirm that sin is in the *flesh!* (Compare Mt. 16:17; I Cor. 15:50). If the mother provides the essential blood-nutrients, the blood must receive the mother's genes! Medically, one's blood can be completely exchanged with blood from a donor, without a change in personality. We think the good doctor is not on firm ground.

Paul says: "Since, therefore, the children [Adam's descendants] share in flesh and blood [Jesus] likewise partook of the *same*…having been made like his brethren *in every respect*" (Heb. 2:14-18): Does this not say that Jesus was a true descendant of Adam, with the identical nature of all human beings? Would Paul agree with Dr. DeHaan that the blood of Jesus came from a source other than the earth? Further, if the "life and blood" of Jesus were not from Mary, how could Jesus be a true descendant of David?

The tract continues: "The sin of Adam was transmitted through the male, not the female: 'By one *man* sin entered into the world' (Rom. 5:12; I Cor. 15:21,22). It was not Eve's sin that was transmitted to the human race but Adam's. It was Adam who was first told not to eat of the forbidden fruit. Sin is reckoned in Adam. Jesus' birth without a human father made him free from Adam's sin."

The above notion is contrary to modern genetics. Both male *and* female are genetic transmitters. Paul said: "There is no difference; *all* have sinned" (Rom. 3:23).

Although God first warned the *man* concerning the forbidden tree, the woman also knew of the prohibition (Gen. 3:3). When she replied to the serpent, she quoted God: "You shall not eat [*tochlu*, plural] of it nor touch [*tig'u*, plural] it lest you die [*t'mutun*, plural]." The prohibition was for both. Indeed, the woman *was* culpable for she was punished.

The above tract claims that Gen. 3:15 foreshadows the "virgin birth": the "woman" is Mary and the "seed" is Jesus. Obviously, the writer is not expert in the Hebrew idiom. Scripture is not alluding to a *specific* woman but *womankind.* Painful childbirth was not only for Eve but *all* women. Surely Christians do not believe that "sinless" Mary, who supposedly conceived by the holy spirit, experienced painful childbirth. Moreover, "seed," although singular, with a singular pronoun, is collective and refers to *all* the woman's descendants. Compare Num. 22:3,5,6, where the singular pronoun means "they."

Matthew cites Isa. 7:14 as foreshadowing the "virgin birth." The Hebrew word traditionally translated as "virgin" is *almah*. The consensus of Biblical scholarship is that *almah* should be translated "young woman."

A careful study of Gen. 24 ("Rebekah at the well") will prove that *almah* means "young woman": Abraham sends his servant to find a wife for Isaac. When the servant reaches Aram-Naharaim, Abraham's birthplace, he rests at a well outside the city. It is evening, the time for water-drawing. Abraham's servant proposes a test by which a bride for Isaac is to be chosen: "The young woman (*naarah*) to whom I say, 'let down your pitcher that I may drink,' and who says, 'drink and I will also water your camels'" is to be the bride of Isaac. That young woman turns out to be Rebekah. She is described as "very beautiful, a *virgin*" (*betulah*). When the servant later recounts the event to Rebekah's brother Laban, instead of *naarah* for "young woman" he uses *almah*, the same Hebrew word used in Isa. 7:14. So here, based on the context, we have *almah* as "young woman" and *betulah* as virgin. Cf. Exod. 2:8; Pr. 30:19; Ps. 68:25 (26); Song 1:3; 6:8.

In the Greek Septuagint translation, *almah* is translated as *parthenos*, the same word used for Dinah after she was raped (Gen. 34:3). "Virgin" in Hebrew is *betulah* (Gen. 24:16; Exod. 22:16 [15]; Lev. 21:14; Ezek. 44:22, etc.). The Hebrew for "young man" is *elem*, as in I Sam. 17:56; 20:22. The "young woman" of Isa. 7:14 is either the wife of King Ahaz, who bore King Hezekiah, or the wife of Isaiah (8:3). Isa. 7:14 is not a messianic prophecy.

The Bible exegete David Kimchi comments: "The birth of a son was given by the prophet as a sign to Ahaz, king of Judah, to convince him of God's promise that he had nothing to fear from the alliance of the kings of Ephraim and Syria who were attacking Jerusalem. If it refers to Jesus 700 years later, how could it convince Ahaz of the truth of Isaiah's prophecy?" Isa. 7:14 is introduced by *hineh*, "behold," which suggests something *about to occur*. (Cf. Isa. 38:8; 39:6,8; Josh. 23:14.) Isaiah speaks of *ha-almah*, "*the* young woman," inferring that the young woman was known to him.

Other than Matthew and Luke, there is no further reference in the Christian Scriptures to the Virgin Birth. Paul says only, "God sent forth his son, born of a woman" (Gal. 4:4). Jesus is never called "Emmanuel."

"EMMANUEL"—"GOD WITH US"

For Trinitarians, "Emmanuel," "God with us," means "God [the son] is with us." But the name "Emmanuel" has no theological overtones. The name of God was often incorporated in the names of Hebrew children as a pious sentiment of gratitude and hope (cf. Gen. 4:1). Cf. Ishmael ("God has heard," Gen. 16:11); Michael ("who is like God"); Samuel ("God has heard"); Elijah ("My God is Jah"); Eliezer ("My God is a helper"); Abijah, Jobab ("Father of God"); Benaiah ("Son of Jah). The altar is called *El-Elohe Yisrael*, "God, the God of Israel" (Gen. 33:20); and *Yahweh-nisi*, "Yahweh is my banner" (Exod. 17:15). Israel and

Jerusalem are called *Yahweh-Tsidkenu,* "Yahweh our righteousness" (Jer. 23:6; 33:16); Jerusalem is also called *Yahweh-shama,* "Yahweh is there" (Ezek. 48:35; Jer. 25:29; cf. Nu. 6:27; Deut. 28:10; II Chron. 7:14; Isa. 44:5; Dan. 9:19).

MORAL IMPLICATIONS OF THE "VIRGIN BIRTH"

Mary and Joseph were espoused to each other (Mt. 1:19,20). The "spirit-impregnation" of Mary violates the sanctity of marriage (Gen. 2:24; Deut. 22:23,24; Mt. 19:5,6) and is contrary to the seventh commandment against adultery (Exod. 20:14). It is reminiscent of the sexual profligacy of the mythological deities (Gen. 6:2-4). Israel was admonished to imitate God's holiness (Deut. 13:4; Lev. 11:44,45; 19:2; 20:26). The spirit-impregnation" of Mary does not commend God's holiness.

THE BIRTH OF ISAAC TO AGED ABRAHAM AND SARAH NO PARALLEL

In an attempt to validate the "virgin birth," Christian theologians cite the example of Abraham and Sarah, who were promised a child in their old age. To still their doubts, they were assured, "Is anything too hard for YHVH?" (Gen. 18:14). Jesus said, "With God all things are possible" (Mt. 19:26; Lu. 1:37; 18:27). However, Paul says, "It is impossible for God to lie" (Heb. 6:18). There is no contradiction. God *can* do all things but will do nothing inconsistent with his nature and revealed will. For example, God cannot be unjust (cf. Gen. 18:25). The "virgin-birth" is inconsistent with God's revealed nature.

We do not reject the "virgin birth" on the grounds of *biological* impossibility. Miracles are reported in Scripture. But we must be careful not to rely on this concept as a blanket justification for every kind of mythological novelty. Tenuous interpretations of isolated proof-texts should not determine important religious teachings. It is remarkable that a doctrine so crucial to Christianity as the "virgin birth" has such slim Scriptural support. Aside from the original birth accounts in Matthew and Luke, the Christian Scriptures never again refer to it!

Abraham and Sarah are no argument for the "virgin birth." The "miracle" of Isaac's birth to the aged Abraham and Sarah is in the category of the great ages attributed to early Biblical personalities. Whereas there is a moral question regarding God's alleged impregnation of a betrothed virgin, there is no question of morality with regard to Abraham and Sarah bearing a child in their old age.

WRONG GENEALOGY FOR JESUS

To authenticate Jesus' messiahship, his ancestry is traced to King David, through Joseph (Lu. 1:27; 2:4). But this genealogy is invalid since Joseph was not Jesus' biological father. Some have attempted to reconcile this by suggesting that Joseph adopted Jesus. But Jewish law makes no provision for legal adoption nor can there be any substitution for the biological father in matters of descent. Moreover, since Jesus was supposedly the "son of God," there could be no paternal line. The genealogy of Mary is not given because Hebrew royal lineage was paternal. Paul likens Jesus to Melchizedek who was "without father or mother or genealogy" (Heb. 7:3). Is Paul attempting to de-emphasize Jesus' genealogy? (Note: Mary's kinswoman Elizabeth is "of the daughters of Aaron"—a Levite (Lu. 1:5,36). But of Mary's tribal origin we know nothing! For Jesus to descend from David, Mary would have to be of the tribe of Judah.)

JESUS DID NOT FULFILL "MESSIANIC" PROPHECIES

Jesus said, "Everything written of me in the law of Moses and the prophets and the Psalms must be fulfilled" (Lu. 24:44). But all was not fulfilled! The angel prophesied that Jesus would rule on the throne of David, over the house of Jacob forever (Isa. 9:6,7). Jesus did *not* receive the "throne of David"—an *earthly* throne. Jesus claimed his kingdom was "not of this world" and denied being "king of the Jews" (Jn. 18:336; cf. Mt. 2:2,6; Mk. 1:15; 11:10; Lu. 1:32,33,54,68,71). In fact, he seems even to deny Davidic lineage (Mt. 22:41-46; Mk. 12:35-37; Lu. 20:41-44)!

Jesus did not establish a world government of endless peace. Nor was a *heavenly* kingdom meant, for the heavenly kingdom already existed (I Chron. 29:11; Ps. 103:19; 145:13; cf. Mt. 6:13). The argument that Jesus brought peace to the hearts of believers is not applicable. Such peace was already available to God's people (Ps. 119:165). The peace Messiah was to bring would be universal, affecting all nations, not just believers (Ps. 86:9; Isa. 52:10; 60:3; 66:23; Dan. 2:44; 7:27; Zeph. 3:9; Zech. 9:10).

ONLY ONE "MOST HIGH"

Messiah was to "reign over the house of Jacob forever." This was not fulfilled. The Jews have never accepted Jesus as their Messiah, although it was prophesied, "Your people shall be willing in the day of Your power" (Ps. 110:3). Jesus was to "save his people from their sins." Where is the evidence that Jesus did this? On the contrary, Jews have suffered greatly at the hands of the so-called followers of Jesus. Moreover, salvation was available to the Jewish People prior to Jesus' coming (Cf. Isa. 1:18; 43:12). If it is argued that Jesus did indeed "save his people from their sins," i.e., his faithful followers, we see no evidence of this. "Believers" still are capable of sinning!

Jesus is called "son of the Most High" (Mk. 5:7; Lu. 1:32,35,76). This contradicts the Trinity: The "second person" of the Trinity is called "God the Son" and is supposedly "co-equal" with God the Father. If Jesus is the "Son of the *Most High*," he cannot be *equal* with "God the Father". There can be only *one* "Most High."

"A PROPHET LIKE MOSES"

In support of Jesus' messiahship, Peter quotes from Deuteronomy 18: "Moses said, 'The Lord God will raise up for you a prophet from your brethren as he raised me up. You shall listen to him in whatever he tells you. And it shall be that every soul that does not listen to that prophet shall be destroyed from the people'" (Acts 3:22,23). But the original quote has more: "I will raise up for them a prophet *like you* from among their brethren; and *I will put my words in his mouth*, and he shall speak to them all that I command them. And whoever will not give heed to my words which *he shall speak in my name*, I myself will require it of him. But the prophet who presumes to speak a word in my name which I have not commanded him to speak, or who speaks in the name of other gods, that same prophet shall die...When a prophet speaks in the name of YHVH, if the word does not come to pass or come true, that is a word which YHVH has not spoken; the prophet has spoken presumptuously." Peter's omissions are critical: The future prophet is not to speak *in his own name*! Moses ministered "in the name of YHVH" (Deut. 18:5) and was punished when he neglected to do so (Nu. 20:10-12; cf. Gen. 40:8; 41:16,25, where Joseph dutifully credits God). Despite his claim that he spoke by God's authority (Jn. 5:19; 8:28; 12:49), Jesus repeatedly said, "I say unto you." Jesus taught that prayer should be offered in *his name* (Jn. 14:13; 15:16; 16:23). By contrast, the prophets of old spoke in God's name— "thus says the Lord." The promised Messiah was to "feed his flock in the strength of YHVH, *in the majesty of the name of YHVH his God*" (Micah 5:4; cf. Isa. 65:16; Ezek. 13:2,3).

The future prophet would be "like Moses." He would be raised up"—chosen from *among his brethren*. This does not at all suggest "virgin birth." The prophet is not supernatural, not an "incarnation" of a heavenly being. He is human, a servant of YHVH" (Josh. 1:1), like Moses.

Jesus assumes divine prerogatives, appropriating the very name by which God revealed himself to Moses: "Truly, truly, I say to you, before Abraham was, *I am*" (Jn. 8:58; cf. Exod. 3:14). "I am the way, and the truth, and the life; no one comes to the Father but by me...He who has seen me has seen the Father...I am the resurrection and the life...I am the light of the world" (Jn. 14:6,9; 11:25; 8:12). "The Son of man has authority on earth to forgive sins" (Mt. 9:6). "All power in heaven and on earth has been given to me...No one knows the Son except the Father, and no one knows the Father except the Son, and any one to whom the Son chooses to reveal him...Hereafter, you will see the Son of man seated on the right hand of Power, and coming on the clouds of heaven" (Mt. 11:27; 28:18; 26:64).

According to Acts, "God foretold by the mouth of all his prophets that his Christ should suffer" (Acts 3:18). The suffering and crucifixion of Jesus, however, are quite *unlike* Moses: "The prophets, neither in the original passages nor in the Jewish interpretation of them 'foretold...that his Christ should suffer .' For even the 'suffering servant' prophecies were never interpreted messianically" (Interpreter's *Bible*, Acts, p. 59). Cf. Isa. 9:6,7, which contains no hint of suffering.

Who, then, was the "future prophet like Moses?" As Moses was "the servant of YHVH," (Josh. 1:1; 8:30), Joshua likewise is called "the servant of YHVH" (24:29).

"SON OF GOD"

Jesus is called the "only son of God" (Mt. 26:63,64; Jn. 1:14,18; 3:16-18; 10:36; Rom. 8:3,32; Gal. 4:4; 1 Jn. 4:9). But Adam also was called "son of God" (Lu. 3:38). Paul applies Ps. 2:7 to Jesus: "YHVH said to me, 'You are my son, this day I have begotten you'" (Acts 13:33). But this poses a problem for trinitarians. The "second person" of the Trinity, "God the son," is said to be "eternally begotten." However, if the son of Ps. 2:7 is begotten on a *certain* day, he cannot be "eternal." Cf. Col. 1:15, where Jesus is called "the first-born of all creation." Ps 2:7 is addressed to the king of Israel (v. 6). The expression, "this day I have begotten you," symbolizes enthronement (Cf. II Sam. 7:12–14; I Chron. 22:10, which refer to king Solomon). Of David God says: "He shall cry to me, 'You are my Father'...I will make him the first-born, the highest of the kings of the earth" (Ps. 89:26,27). Being made "first-born" symbolizes being anointed king (v. 20). The "kings of the earth" are the local kings—the kings of Philistia, etc. (Jer . 25:20).

Israel is God's "son" and "first-born" (Exod. 4:22; Deut. 14:1; 26:18; Ps. 135:4; Isa. 63:16; Jer. 3:19; 31:9,20; Hos. 11:1; 1:10). The angels as well as humans are "sons of God" (Gen. 6:2; Job 1:6; Mal. 2:10).

According to the Trinity, Jesus, as "god the son," is "co-eternal" and "co-omnipotent" with the Father (Jn. 1:1). Before his death, Jesus prayed, "Father...glorify your son with the glory I had with you before the world was made" (Jn. 17:1,5). But he who grants glory is greater than he who receives it— no "co-omnipotence." Paul said of Jesus: [He] was designated son of God in *power*...by his resurrection from the dead" (Rom. 1:4). Because Jesus *receives power* at his resurrection, he could not have been *eternally* co-omnipotent" with "God the Father."

At his resurrection, Jesus sat down at the right hand of the Majesty on high" (Heb. 1:3; 8:1; 10:12; 12:2; 1 Pet. 3:22). Jesus is not seated on the central throne of supremacy but in the subordinate right-hand position—no "co-omnipotence"! Although the Trinity posits "three persons in one," here there are two distinct persons. Where is the "third person" of the Trinity? In Job, when the sons of God present themselves before YHVH (Job 1:6; 2:1), where are the "second and third persons" of the Trinity? Where is the "Logos" who allegedly was "with God" (Jn. 1:1) and shared God's glory (Jn. 17:5)?

How did the "eternally begotten son," "second person" of the Trinity, become a "son"? Was it through some procreative act in heaven? Jesus' claim to be the only son of God is presumptuous, pagan, and contrary to monotheism.

"BESIDES ME THERE IS NO SAVIOR"

The name *Yeshua* (Jesus) is ever on the lips of "Messianic Jews." They follow Paul who said: "I decided to know nothing among you save Jesus Christ and him crucified" (I Cor. 2:2). With Peter, they fervently believe there is no other name under heaven...by which we must be saved" (Acts 4:12). In glorifying Jesus, "Messianic Jews" go counter to God's declaration: "I, even I, am YHVH, and *besides me there is no savior*" (Isa. 43:11).

"Messianic Jews" teach that "Yeshua"-Jesus means "salvation." However, the Hebrew for "salvation" is *Y'shuah*, which ends in the Hebrew letter *heh*. If we may take "midrashic" (allegorical, metaphorical) liberty, the Hebrew letter *heh* in Judaism stands for *hashem*, "the name," the ineffable name YHVH. Jesus is but a man, not God—the *heh* is missing: "They pray to a god that cannot save" (Isa. 45:20; cf. Deut. 29:25,26).

THE "JEWISHNESS" OF JESUS

"Messianic Jews" make much of the "Jewishness" of Jesus. Jesus said to the Pharisees, "In *your* law it is written" (Jn. 8:17; cf. 15:25) and, "*Your* father Abraham" (Jn. 8:56). In thus speaking, Jesus disassociates himself from the Jewish people. If Jesus was an "observant" Jew, why does he omit the Sabbath commandment (Mt. 19:17-19)? It is also noteworthy that Jesus is never referred to as a "Jew." (The Gospel-writer likewise betrays his non-alliance with the Jews in saying, "the Passover of *the Jews*," "*the Jews*' feast of Tabernacles", etc. (Jn. 2:13; 7:2; 11:55).

The critical issue is not whether Jesus was a Jew *biologically* but whether he was a Jew *religiously* and how he is perceived by his followers? Christians do not think of Jesus as a Jew. Jesus frequented the synagogue (Lu. 4:16), not to pray with his Jewish brethren, but to preach to them—much the same as present-day "Messianic Jews" visit synagogues seeking opportunities to missionize Jews.

FOR JEWS ONLY *ONE* NAME

For Jews there is only one name: "If they will diligently learn the ways of my people, to swear by *my name*, 'As *YHVH* lives', even as they taught my people to swear by Baal, then they shall be built up in the midst of my people" (Jer. 12:16). "Blessed is the man who trusts in YHVH [not "Yeshua"]" (Jer. 17:17). Concerning those who would distract the Children of Israel from their Creator, Jeremiah says: "Who think to cause my people to forget my name by their dreams which they tell one another, as their fathers forgot my name for Baal" (Jer. 26:26,27). Jer. 31:31-34 is a favorite reference of missionaries to prove the replacement of the "Old Covenant" by the "New." However, they have over-looked an important element. In the messianic era, "No longer shall each man teach his neighbor and each his brother, saying 'Know *Yahweh*' for they shall all know me." Where is "Yeshua"?

*   *   *

According to Deut. 18:15-22, a true prophet is known by the fulfillment of his prophecies. In a later chapter we shall examine the prophecies alleged to have been fulfilled in Jesus.

CHAPTER 6

HOLY SPIRIT

RUACH HAKODESH

The theology of "Messianic Judaism" shares much in common with Pentecostalism, with its emphasis on the "outpouring of the holy spirit," divine healing, and "speaking in tongues." Together with most Christians, "Messianic Jews" believe the "holy spirit," which they call *ruach* h*akodesh*, to be the third person of the Trinity—"God the holy spirit."

We first encounter the spirit of God—*ruach Elohim*—in Genesis 1:2: "And the spirit of God was hovering over the surface of the water." The account does not say, "the holy spirit," but "the spirit of God." The difference is significant. The expression, "the holy spirit," might suggest an independent entity, whereas "spirit *of* God" is a *possession* of God, an emanation from him. In our text the creative energy of God is poised above the waters, precedent to the creative act. The spirit is not a deity, but an impersonal force, emanating from God—the divine presence, as it were. God is the sole Creator: "In the beginning *God* created" (Gen. 1:1). "By his spirit he beautified the heavens" (Job 26:13). "The spirit of God made me and the breath of the Almighty gave me life" (Job 33:4). The spirit is not an independent deity but *belongs to* God. *Ruach*, "spirit," is almost always feminine, and indeed, in Gen. 1:2, has a feminine verb—*m'rachefet*, "hovering." Would Trinitarians be willing to grant feminine status to the third person of the Trinity?

The expression, "the holy spirit," *ruach hakodesh*, as "Messianic Jews" refer to it, does not occur in this form in Scripture. The following forms, however, do occur:

"The spirit of God" (*ruach Elohim*) (Gen. 1:2; Exod. 31:3; 35:31; Num. 24:2; I Sam. 19:20, 23). "The spirit of YHVH" (*ruach YHVH*) (Judg. 3:10; 11:29; 13:25; 14:6,19; 15:14; I Sam. 10:6,10; 11:6; 16:13,14; II Sam. 23:2; Isa. 11:2; 40:7,13; 61:1; Ezek. 11:5). "The spirit of God" (*ruach El*) (Job 33:4). "My spirit" (*ruchi*) (Hag. 2:5). "His spirit" (*rucho*) (Isa. 48:16). "Your holy spirit" (*ruach kodshechah*) (Ps. 51:11 [H. 13]). "His holy spirit" (*ruach kodsho*) (Isa. 63:10,11). In all of these, the spirit is *of* God—his possession. What *belongs* to God cannot be *equal* to God.

But what of Isaiah 48:16: "The Lord (*Adonai*) GOD (*YHVH*) has sent me and his spirit."? The meaning is not that two entities sent Isaiah, as Trinitarians suggest. The spirit of God is subject *to* God, is an element *of* God. Isaiah 48:16 could be paraphrased, "The Lord sent me *by* his spirit." Cf. Zech. 7:12: "...which YHVH of hosts sent by his spirit (*shalach...b'rucho*) by the hand of the former prophets." Immediately following our passage we read: "Thus says YHVH your Redeemer, the Holy One of Israel: 'I am YHVH your God who teaches you to profit, who leads you in the way you should go.'" The focus is on *God*. Compare also Zech. 4:6, "by my spirit."

Trinitarians cite Isa. 63:10: "They rebelled and grieved his holy spirit." Trinitarian interpretation: The "holy spirit" is "grieved," therefore is a person. But what is *his* can not be his equal; what is possessed can never equal the possessor. The correct meaning is, "They grieved his heart," as in Gen. 6:6: "And it grieved his heart that he had made man;" and Judg. 10:16: "His soul was grieved for the misery of Israel." Or, one could say simply, "They grieved him," as in Ps. 78:40: "How often did they rebel against him in the wilderness; they grieved him in the desert." If I say, "You have grieved my heart," I certainly do not imply that my heart is an entity separate from me. The inference is, "You have grieved me." To "grieve the spirit of" is a Hebraism (cf. Ps. 106:33; Isa. 54:6).

"Holy spirit" appears nowhere in the Tanach in this form and the declined form—"your holy spirit" and "his holy spirit"—appear only twice. Compared to this, the divine name YHVH appears over 6000 times!

The Psalmist prayed, "Create for me a pure heart, O God, and renew within me a right spirit. Cast me not away from your presence and take not your holy spirit from me" (Ps. 51:11, 12 [H. 12, 13]). "Where shall I go from your spirit and where shall I flee from your presence?" (Ps. 139:7). God's spirit in man denotes God's presence. God may infuse us with his spirit or remove it. The spirit is not a Trinitarian entity acting independently of God. Because God is invisible and infinite, of necessity, we speak of God's *spirit* being in us rather than *God* being in us. For example: we speak of the sun's rays warming us; but the rays are not an independent entity but an extension of the sun.

Joel prophesied: "You shall know that I am in the midst of Israel, and that I, YHVH, am your God and there is none else. And my people shall never again be put to shame. And it shall come to pass afterward, that I will pour out my spirit on all flesh; your sons and your daughters shall prophesy, your old men shall dream dreams, and your young men shall see visions" (Joel 2:27,28). The words of Joel are often misunderstood. The promise is to *Israel*, "all flesh" meaning every Israelite—young and old. *God* is the principle actor. It is He who pours out *his* spirit; the spirit is not autonomous.

In a book dealing with the holy spirit, a Pentecostal evangelist writes: "Jehovah is the name of the triune being—not the name of just one of them. The Father is Jehovah. The son is Jehovah. The Holy Ghost is Jehovah." This trinitarian statement contradicts the following Scriptures:

"And they shall know that you, your name is YHVH; *you alone* are the most high over all the earth" (Ps. 83:18 [19]). (The triple usage of the second-person pronoun is striking, as though God's uniqueness were being challenged by an imaginary disputant.)

"I am YHVH, that is my name; and my glory to another I shall not give, nor my praise to graven images" (Isa. 42:8). Again, note the emphasis on God's exclusiveness.

"And YHVH shall be king over all the earth. On that day YHVH shall be one and *his name one*" (Zech. 14:9).

The assertion, than, that "Jehovah is the name of the triune being not the name of just one of them" flies in the face of Scripture!

Finally, we would ask: If the "holy spirit" is the third-person deity of the Trinity, co-equal with the father and the son, why, in the countless places in Christian Scripture where father and son are mentioned, is the "holy spirit" absent? For example, "One God the Father and one lord Jesus Christ" (I Cor. 8:6) or, "I and the Father are one" (Jn. 10:30; 17:21,22). In the formulaic greetings at the beginning of the epistles, the "holy spirit" is not mentioned together with God and Jesus. (Rom. 1:7; 15:6; II Cor. 1:2,3; 11:31; Gal. 1:1,3,10; Eph. 1:2,3; Php. 1:2; Col. 1:3; I Thess. 1:1; II Thess. 1:1; I Tim. 1:1,2; II Tim. 1:2; Tit. 1:1,4; Philem. 3.)

To seek support in the Hebrew Scriptures for the trinitarian doctrine of the holy spirit is futile. The Trinity is unscriptural. Rather, the pages of the Tanach breathe Monotheism throughout: "YHVH is one…there is no other beside him Who is like you, O YHVH?…Make no mention of other gods…I am he and there is no god beside me…There is none holy like YHVH…You are the God, you alone . For God alone my soul waits in silence…Whom have I in heaven but you...Let them praise the name of YHVH; for his name alone is exalted...To whom then will you liken God I am YHVH who made all things—Who was with me? In that day shall YHVH be one and his name one.' (See chapter, GOD IS ONE, NOT THREE.)

CHAPTER 7

MESSIAH

The Christian Scriptures freely quote from the Hebrew Scriptures, the typical formula being, "that it might be fulfilled which was spoken by…" (Mt. 1:22, etc.). The reader compares "prophecy" and "fulfillment" and is "convinced," not realizing that the "fulfillment" may have been fictionalized to conform to the prophecy. This may be compared to a pre-shot arrow around which a target is drawn to make it appear that the arrow has hit its mark. Certain details in the life of Jesus might be "verified" by this method, but it cannot work for recorded and observable history. The messianic prophecy of universal peace, for example, cannot be fictionalized.

"MASHIACH"

"Messiah" is from the Hebrew *mashiach*, an adjective meaning "anointed" (with oil), and by implication, "chosen." The high priest and/or king was called "*m'shiach-YHVH*," "anointed of the Lord" (Lev. 4:3; I Sam. 24:6,10; 26:9,11,16,23). Israel was called "God's anointed" or *mashiach* (Ps. 84:9 [10]; 89:38,51 [39,52]; 105:15; I Chron. 16:22; Lam. 4:20; Hab. 3:13). When the king or priest was inducted into office, he was anointed with oil (Ps. 89:20). "Messiah," as *world leader* and *savior*, is post-Biblical. In Hebrew Scripture, God alone is the Savior (I Sam. 12:12).

CHRISTIAN MESSIAH DOES NOT FIT DAVIDIC PROTOTYPE

The prototype of the Messiah, both in Judaism and Christianity, is King David. Isa. 9:6,7, one of the most oft-quoted messianic passages, speaks of the coming ruler's endless government of peace as being established "on the throne of David." (For further discussion, see "Messianic Passages.") God's night-revelation to the prophet Nathan directed to David is most instructive: "Go and speak to my servant, to David...'I took you from the pasture, from following the sheep, to be a prince over my people, over Israel. And I was with you wherever you went and have cut off all your enemies from before you; and I have made you a great name like the name of the great ones in the land. And I will establish a place for my people Israel and I will plant them and they shall dwell in their own place and move no more; neither shall the children of wickedness afflict them any more, as at first...And when your days are fulfilled and you shall lie down with your fathers, I will establish your seed after you who shall proceed from your bowels, and I will make his kingdom secure. He will build a house for my name and I will establish the throne of his kingdom forever. I will be a father to him and he will be a son to me. If he commits iniquity, I will chasten him with the rod of men, and with the stripes of the children of men. But my mercy shall not leave him'" (II Sam. 7:4-15).

What are the key elements in the above "messianic profile"? Israel will no longer be oppressed but shall dwell securely in its own land. The Davidic heir will build a house for God. The relationship of God and the king will be like father and son. If the king sins, he will be chastened but God's mercy will never leave him. What is missing from this profile is significant: Messiah is not super-human or divine. He is a fallible, mortal human being. There is no sacrificial, atoning death. The theological Jesus does not fit this profile.

MESSIAH BRINGS UNIVERSAL PEACE

Messiah's mission is universal peace and justice (Jer. 23:5). When the birth of Jesus was announced, it was said: "Glory to God in the highest, and on earth peace" (Lu. 2:14). Messiah, the "Prince of Peace" (Isa. 9:6), causes war to cease: "They shall beat their swords into plowshares, and their spears into pruning hooks; nation shall not lift up sword against nation, neither shall they learn war any more" (Isa. 2:4; Mic. 4:3). "He shall command peace to the nations; his dominion shall be from sea to sea, and from the River to the ends of the earth" (Zech. 9:10). Under Messiah, families are brought together: "Behold, I will send you Elijah the prophet before the great and terrible day of YHVH comes. And he will turn the hearts of fathers to their children and the hearts of children to their fathers" (Mal. 4:5,6). But contrast this messianic picture of peace with Jesus' words: "I have not come to bring peace, but a sword...a man's foes will be those of his own household" (Mt. l0:34–36; Lu. 12:51–53). Jesus' appearance did not result in universal peace.

MESSIAH ENDS FEAR AND VIOLENCE

"A bruised reed he will not break, and a dimly burning wick he will not quench; he will faithfully bring forth justice. He will not fail or be discouraged till he has established justice in the earth...With righteousness he shall judge the poor, and decide with equity for the meek of the earth...The wolf shall dwell with the lamb, and the leopard shall lie down with the kid, and the calf and the lion and fatling together, and a little child shall lead them. The cow and the bear shall feed; their young shall lie down together; and the lion shall eat straw like the ox...They shall not hurt or destroy in all my holy mountain; for the earth shall be full of the knowledge of YHVH as the waters cover the sea" (Isa. 42:3,4; 11:4–9; 65:25). It is not just the "faithful few" who know God but the entire earth. Fear is eliminated: "Every man shall sit under his vine and under his fig tree, and none shall make them afraid" (Mic. 4:4). Suffering and sadness cease: "No more shall be heard in it the sound of weeping and the cry of distress" (Isa. 65:19). Jesus did not end fear and violence.

"ALL FLESH SHALL COME TO WORSHIP"

Messiah's rule affects the entire world, not just "believers": "YHVH has bared his holy arm before the eyes of all the nations; and all the ends of the earth shall see the salvation of our God" (Isa. 52:10; See also Isa. 11:10; 42:6; 49:6; 60:3; 61:11; 66:23; Jer. 3:17; Ps. 2:8; 86:9; 98:3; Dan. 7:27; Zeph. 3:9; Lu. 3:6). "In you shall all the nations of the earth be blessed" (Gen. 12:3; 18:18; 22:18; 26:4). "In the days of those kings the God of heaven will set up a kingdom which shall never be destroyed" (Dan. 2:44). "YHVH will judge the ends of the earth; he will give strength to his king, and exalt the power of his anointed" (I Sam. 2:10).

Messiah is not impotent at his coming, nor must he await a "second coming" to confirm his kingdom: "Many peoples and strong nations shall come to seek YHVH of hosts in Jerusalem...His dominion shall be from sea to sea, and from the River to the ends of the earth" (Zech. 8:22; 9:10; cf. Mt. 21:5).

Messiah's coming is the year of YHVH's favor, of world-redemption: "The spirit of the Lord YHVH is upon me, because YHVH has anointed me to bring good tidings to the afflicted, he has sent me to bind up the brokenhearted, to proclaim liberty to the captives, and the opening of the prison to those who are bound; to proclaim the year of YHVH's favor, and the day of vengeance of our

God; to comfort *all* who mourn" (Isa. 61:1,2). Jesus quotes this, adding: "Today this Scripture is fulfilled in your hearing" (Lu. 4:18–21). But it was *not* fulfilled! The world remains unredeemed

"JUDAH WILL BE SAVED, ISRAEL WILL DWELL SECURELY"

Messiah redeems Israel: "In those days Judah will be saved, and Israel will dwell securely" (Jer. 23:6; 33:16.) Christians would interpret "Judah" and" Israel" as "believing Christians"—the "Israel of God" (Gal 6:16). But this is unwarranted, as indicated by Jer. 23:3: "You shall know that I am in the midst of Israel, and that I YHVH, am your God and there is none else. And my people shall never again be put to shame...For behold, in those days and at that time, when I restore the fortunes of Judah and Jerusalem, I will gather all the nations and bring them down to the valley of Jehoshaphat, and I will enter into judgment with them there, on account of my people and my heritage Israel, because they have scattered them among the nations, and have divided up my land...But YHVH is a refuge to his people, a stronghold to the people Israel...And Jerusalem shall be holy and strangers shall never again pass through it...I will avenge their blood, and I will not clear the guilty, for YHVH dwells in Zion" (Joel 2:27; 3:1,2,16,17,21; Zeph. 3:15,20). "My servant David shall be king over them; and they shall all have one shepherd. They shall follow my ordinances and be careful to observe my statutes. They shall dwell in the land where your fathers dwelt that I gave to my servant Jacob; they and their children and their children's children shall dwell there forever; and *David my servant* shall be their prince forever. I will make a covenant of peace with them; it shall be an everlasting covenant with them; and I will bless them and multiply them, and will set my sanctuary in the midst of them forevermore. My dwelling place shall be with them; and I will be their God, and they shall be my people. Then the nations will know that I YHVH sanctify Israel, when my sanctuary is in the midst of them forevermore" (Ezek. 37:23–28; 34:23,24; 36:24–28; 39:29; Mic. 5:4)..."Behold, I will save my people from the east country and from the west country; and I will bring them to dwell in the midst of Jerusalem; and they shall be my people and I will be their God, in faithfulness and in righteousness...On that day YHVH their God will save them for they are the flock of his people; for like the jewels of a crown they shall shine on his land" (Zech. 8:7,8; 9:16).

"HE WILL ASSEMBLE THE OUTCASTS OF ISRAEL"

"He will raise an ensign for the nations, and will assemble the outcasts of Israel, and gather the dispersed of Judah from the four corners of the earth" (Isa. 11:12). "The children of Israel shall return and seek YHVH their God, and

David their king" (Hos. 3:5; cf. Jer. 30:9) (God and Messiah-David are two distinct beings—one superior and one subordinate. They are not a "Trinity." Cf. I Tim. 6:13.)]. "Then the offering of Judah and Jerusalem will be pleasing to YHVH as in the days of old and as in former years" (Mal. 3:4). The Christian messiah did not redeem Israel.

TESTIMONY OF CHRISTIAN SCRIPTURES THAT MESSIAH WILL "HELP ISRAEL" AND RULE OVER IT

Jesus was to "save his people from their sins" (Mt. 1:20,21). Mary prayed: "He has helped his servant Israel" (Lu. 1:54,55). Zechariah, the father of John the Baptist, prayed: "Blessed be the Lord God of Israel, for He has visited and redeemed his people..." (Lu. 1:67-74; cf. Lu. 2:25-32).). Messiah was to "reign over the house of Jacob" (Mt. 2:6; Lu. 1:33). But the Jewish people were not helped or redeemed by Jesus nor did he rule over them. To the contrary, Israel has been the world's sacrificial lamb, culminating in the horror of the Nazi holocaust.

When the Jews did not accept Jesus' "kingship," the message of Christianity was extended to the Gentiles: "It was necessary that the word of God should be spoken first to you [the Jews]. Since you thrust it from you, and judge yourselves unworthy of eternal life, behold, we turn to the Gentiles. For the Lord has commanded us, saying, 'I have set you to be a light for the Gentiles, that you may bring salvation to the uttermost parts of the earth'" (Acts 13:46,47). Paul inaccurately quotes from Isa. 49:6 and 42:6: "It is too light a thing that you should be my servant to raise up the tribes of Jacob and to restore the preserved of Israel; I will give you as a light to the nations, that my salvation may reach to the end of the earth I have given you as a covenant to the people, a light to the nations, to open the eyes that are blind, to bring out the prisoners from the dungeon, from the prison those who sit in darkness." *Isaiah* is the "light," whose message of divine salvation dispels the darkness and blindness—the misery and despondency—of the "nations," the "tribes of Jacob," who have been taken captive by the Babylonian-Chaldeans (Isa. 11:12).

MESSIAH NOT REJECTED BY HIS OWN

Paul's scenario is wrong: Messiah redeems *Israel*, then the world. God's message is not offered to the Gentiles as an alternative to and consequence of Israel's alleged unworthiness. Messiah is not rejected by his own: "To him shall be the obedience of the peoples" (Gen. 49:10). "Your people shall be willing in the day of your power" (Ps. 110:3). Israel delights in God's messenger of the covenant

(Mal. 3:1). Messiah is sent to *Israel*: "Unto *us* a child is born; unto *us* a child is given" (Isa. 9:6). There is not the slightest hint of Messiah's rejection by Israel.

Messiah rules on the "throne of David" (Isa. 9:7; Jer. 23:5; Ezek. 37:24; Hos. 3:5; Cf. Lu. 1:32, 33). Messiah establishes an *earthly* kingdom—the "throne of David" is not in heaven. The kingdom of heaven pre-exists Messiah's coming and is already at peace (Job 25:2). Messiah's kingdom is established with "judgment and justice"—values needed by suffering and strife-torn humanity. By contrast, the Christian messiah's kingdom is "not of this world" (Jn. 18:36) but is heavenly (Mt. 26:64). Messiah restores the Law of Moses (Mal. 4:4; Isa. 2:2,3; Ps. 132:12).

MESSIAH NEED NOT "COME AGAIN" TO FULFILL HIS MISSION

The Jewish Messiah fulfills his mission without having to "come again." The notion of a "second coming" was introduced when the Christian messiah failed to bring about world-redemption (Jn. 14:28; Mt. ch. 24).

"DAVIDIC DESCENT" FROM JESUS IN QUESTION

Messiah was to be David's descendant (Isa. 9:7; Jer. 23:5). Jesus is called the "son of David" (Mt. 9:27; 20:30; 15:22; Mk. 10:47,48; Lu. 18:38,39). Paul acknowledges Jesus' descent from David (Rom. 1:3) and in Revelation Jesus is called the "root of David" (Rev. 5:5; 22:16). But there is ambiguity concerning his Davidic descent: "As Jesus taught in the temple, he said, 'How can the scribes say that the Christ is the son of David? David himself, inspired by the holy spirit, declared, "The Lord said to my Lord, Sit at my right hand, till I put your enemies under your feet." David himself calls him Lord; so how is he his son?'" (Mk. 12:35,37; Mt. 22:42-45). Peake comments: "Jesus held that Messiah does not depend on Davidic descent for his authority...Either Jesus did not claim to be of the house of David or else...set little value on this connection" (*Peak's* commentary, p. 696).

Although Matthew's Gospel begins, "The book of the genealogy of Jesus Christ, the son of David" (Mt. 1:1), Jesus' Davidic lineage is in doubt. The Jews reckoned legal descent through the father. But the genealogies of Jesus in Matthew and Luke, which trace Jesus' lineage through Joseph, are irrelevant; Joseph was not Jesus' biological father. Mary's genealogy is missing.

SUMMARY

Messiah is Davidic. He rules over redeemed Israel, effects universal peace and justice, restores Mosaic Law, is not rejected by Israel, is universally accepted, does not forgive sin and does not die vicariously. He is not super-human or divine but human and fallible. He needs no "second coming" but fulfills prophecy at his coming. Jesus does not fit this profile.

"The [Jewish] rejection of Jesus as Messiah is fully justifiable since it is an astonishing assumption by Gentile Christians that they are more competent than the Jews to say what the name of Messiah signifies and requires" (Amberly, *Analysis of Religious Belief,* Vol. 1, p. 388 [1876].)

CHAPTER 8

"MESSIANIC" PASSAGES

The following passages are applied by Christian interpreters to Jesus:

"HE SHALL BRUISE YOUR HEAD"

Gen. 3:14,15: "YHVH God said to the serpent: I will put enmity between you and the woman and between your seed and her seed. He will bruise your head and you will bruise his heel." Christian interpretation: The "woman" is Mary, the "seed" is Jesus, and the "serpent" is Satan. Satan "bruises the heel of Jesus"—a non-mortal wound because Jesus retrieves his life by resurrection. Jesus in turn "bruises the head of Satan"—a mortal wound.

But there are problems with the above interpretation. The two antagonists supposedly are Jesus and Satan but the prediction concerns the woman's *seed* and the serpent's *seed*. If the serpent in Eden was Satan, who is Satan's *seed*? Also, whereas Jesus was "bruised" (crucifixion?), where is the "heel-wound" to the serpent's seed? According to the Christian Scriptures, the time of Jesus was the "end-time" and Satan was to have been vanquished "shortly," implying the final end of evil (Rom. 16:20; Heb. 2:14). But evil still exists!

"Seed," *zerah*, as used above in Gen. 3, is a collective noun meaning "descendants" (Gen. 13:16; Isa. 61:9). The singular "he," referring to the seed," is used generically—"mankind": Cf. Num. 22:3,5,6, where "he" means "they." The individuals mentioned in vv. 14–16 represent their respective groups: *all* women will travail in childbirth; *all* snakes will crawl on their bellies, etc. Nor is it unusual to speak of the "woman's seed," for we have a similar expression concerning Sarah in Gen. 17:16.

"IN YOUR SEED SHALL ALL THE NATIONS...BE BLESSED"

Gen. 22:18; 26:4: "In your [Abraham's] seed shall all the nations of the earth be blessed." For Paul, the "seed" is Christ: "Now the promises were made to Abraham and to his offspring. It does not say, 'And to offsprings,' referring to many; but, referring to one, 'and to your offspring,' which is Christ" (Gal. 3:16). Paul misinterprets the Genesis passage. The promise was to the descendants— plural: "I will indeed bless you, and I will multiply your descendants...and by your descendants shall all the nations of the earth bless themselves." Abraham's descendants—Israel—would be the paradigm of blessedness: "By you shall Israel bless, saying, 'May God make you like Ephraim and like Manasseh'" (Gen. 48:20; cf. Jer. 4:2).

"UNTIL SHILOH COME"

Gen. 49:10: "The scepter shall not depart from Judah nor the ruler's staff [others—"a lawgiver"] from between his feet as long as men come to Shiloh [others— (1) "until Shiloh come"; (2) "till he come to Shiloh"; (3) "until that which is his comes";] and to him shall be the obedience of the peoples." Opinions differ regarding the translation of Gen. 49:10, whose original Hebrew is obscure. The construction is similar to that of Gen. 8:22: "While the earth remains, seedtime and harvest, and cold and heat, and summer and winter, and day and night shall not cease." The figure here is one of *permanence.* Likewise, rulership will abide with Judah. Messiah will descend from David (Ps. 132:11, etc.). Lacking a valid genealogy, Jesus does not qualify as the messianic heir of David nor does he establish an earthly kingdom (Jn. 18:36). The dispersed of Israel were not regathered to their land and the nations did not become "obedient."

The Kingdom of Judah ended four centuries before Jesus, when King Zedekiah was taken captive by Nebuchadnezzar and the Temple was destroyed. The Herodians, who were not Judeans, ruled Israel thereafter. If Gen. 49:10 is messianic, it was not fulfilled in Jesus.

"A STAR...OUT OF JACOB"

Nu. 24:17-19: "A star shall go forth from Jacob and a scepter shall arise from Israel and shall smite the corners of Moab and destroy all the sons of Sheth. And Edom shall be a possession and Seir shall be a possession for his enemies..." This is not Jesus but David, who conquered Edom, 2 Sam. 8:13,14; ch. 22. How does

Jesus fit the predictions of military conquest? For more on David's military career, see 2 Sam. 3:18; 5:2; 1 Ki. 1:31; 2 Ki. 8:19; 2 Chron. 13:; Ps. 18:50; 78:70,71; 89: 3,4,20,24,26, 27, 29; 139:10-18.

"YOU ARE MY SON"

Psalm 2: "Why do the nations rage, and the peoples contemplate vanity? The kings of the earth set themselves and the rulers take counsel together against YHVH and against his anointed, saying, 'Let us break their bonds, and cast away their cords from us.' He who sits in the heavens laughs; YHVH has them in derision. Then shall he speak to them in his wrath, and terrify them in his fury, saying, 'I have set my king on Zion, my holy hill.' I will tell of the decree of YHVH: He said to me, '*You are my son, today I have begotten you.* . Now therefore, O kings, be wise; be warned, O rulers of the earth. Serve YHVH with fear, worship purely [*nashku bar*]" [cf. Ps. 24:4: *bar levav* ="pure heart"; Gen. 41:10: "By the [word] of your mouth shall my people serve" (*v'al picha yishak kol ami).]* The Authorized Version translates v. 11 as "kiss the son," a much-favored reference of missionaries, with its obvious christological implications. If the Psalmist had wanted to use "son," he would have used *ben*, as in v. 7, not the Aramaic *bar*. But even if the Psalmist *had* intended "son," we have no problem with this for David was called God's son. The Hebrew of v. 12 is considered by both Jewish and Christian scholars to be defective and difficult of reconstruction. The Septuagint translates *nashku bar* as, "accept correction." A symbolic act of submission is suggested (cf. I Sam. 10:1).

The application of Psalm 2 to Jesus (Acts 13:33; Heb. 1:5; 5:5) is unwarranted. The object of the rulers' conspiracy is not an individual but a plurality—"*their* bonds, *their* cords—Israel, God's anointed (I Chron. 16:22; Ps. 28:8; 105:15; Hab. 3:13). King David also is "God's anointed" (I Sam. 12:3; 16:13; 24:6; 2 Sam. 5:17; 2 Chron. 6:42; Ps. 18:50; 89:20; 132:10).

The "begotten son" is David the king: "He shall cry to me, 'You are my Father'. . and I will make him the first-born, the highest of the kings of the earth" (Ps. 89:20,26,27). Solomon also is called God's son: "He shall build a house for my name, and I will establish the throne of his kingdom forever. *I will be his father, and he shall be my son"* (II Sam. 7:13,14). To be "begotten of God" as "first-born" signifies being chosen for the highest office, king of Israel. It is not a "supernatural" begetting in the Christian sense. (Israel also is called God's "first-born son" [Exod. 4:22]).

If the "son" of Psalm 2 is applied to Jesus, Trinitarians have a problem: How can the "second person" of the Trinity be *"eternally* begotten" if he is begotten on a certain day? (Cf. also Prov. 8:22, applied in Christian theology to Jesus and see our discussion above.)

"MY GOD, MY GOD, WHY HAVE YOU FORSAKEN ME?"

Psalm 22: "My God, my God, why have you forsaken me? For you took me from the womb, kept me safe upon my mother's breasts. Upon you was I cast from the womb; from my mother's stomach you are my God…For dogs surround me; the assembly of the wicked encompass me, like a lion [they maul (cf. v. 22; Isa. 38:13)] my hands and my feet…They divide my clothes among them, and for my garment cast lots…I will tell your name to my brethren; in the midst of the congregation I will praise you…All the ends of the earth shall remember and turn to YHVH…for dominion belongs to YHVH, and he rules over the nations."

Christian interpretation: Psalm 22 foreshadows the crucifixion (Mt. 27:46; Mk. 15:34; Mt. 27:35; Mk. 15:24; Lu. 23:34; Jn. 19:24). If this is so, why did Jesus, the so-called "god-man," lose faith? If the answer is that it was the "human" Jesus, we reply: But Jesus, in order to provide the "ransom sacrifice," had to be "blameless" (Mt. 20:28; I Tim. 2:6; Heb. 4:15; 7:26). Jesus, who chided others for their "little faith" (Mt. 6:30; 8:26), was himself lacking in faith!

Psalm 22:9,10 is said to anticipate the Virgin Birth. But there is no hint of a "pre-human" existence (Cf. Jn. 8:58). "Being taken from the womb" means being dedicated to God's service from birth, as with Samson and Samuel (Judg. 13:5,7; 16:17; I Sam. 1:21-28). Psalm 22 is not an allusion to "divine fathering."

"From my mother's stomach, you are my God (not my *father*]" (Ps. 22:.10).

"For dominion belongs to *YHVH* [not to the *child*] and *he* [God, not the child] rules over the nations" (Ps. 22:.28).

What of Ps. 22:16, translated in Christian Bibles, "They have pierced my hands and feet"? The Hebrew is, "*ki s'va-vu-ni k'lavim a-dat m're-im—hi-ki-fu ka-ari ya-dai v'rahg-lai.*" The literal meaning is: "For dogs have encircled me—the assembly of the wicked has surrounded me—as a lion my hands and my feet." The elliptical word probably is "mauled," or "attacked." V. 13 is a parallel: "*Pah-tsu a-lai pi-hem ar-yeh to-ref v'sho-eg,*—"They have opened their mouths against me—a ravening, roaring lion." As in v. 16, v.13 also contains an ellipsis. The Jewish Bible exegete David Kimchi (1160–1235) is critical of those who corrupt *ka-ari* ("like a lion") to read *ka-ru* ("they dug"='they pierced').

"All the world shall turn to YHVH." This was not fulfilled in Jesus. Moreover, the universal "turning to YHVH" precludes the necessity of any "second coming."

"The suffering servant" of Ps. 22 does not die and certainly is not crucified.

"YOUR THRONE, O GOD..."

Ps. 45:6: "Your throne is of God forever and ever. Missionaries apply this to the "second person" of the Trinity. The addressee, however, is the king of Israel, who rules by God's authority. I Chron. 29:23 is analogous: "Solomon sat on the throne of YHVH as king." The everlasting character of his kingdom has no supernatural implications. Of the future royal son of David, Solomon, God said: "I will establish his throne forever" (1 Chron 17:12,14; cf. 2 Sam. 7:16; Ps. 89:4,29,36). The context of Ps. 45:6 indicates that the addressee is not divine but human: His beauty excels all other men (v. 2); He is blessed by God (v. 2); he is anointed by *his God* (v. 7). Messiah's ruling authority, as with the kings of Israel, derives from God: Messiah is not God but is *subject to God*, his anointer. Ps. 45:6 is not trinitarian.

"GIVE THE KING YOUR JUDGMENTS, THE KING'S SON YOUR RIGHTEOUSNESS"

The following is said of Solomon: "God, give the king your judgments and the king's son your righteousness. May he judge your people with righteousness and your poor with judgment...In his days may the righteous flourish and abundant peace as long as the moon endures. May he rule from sea to sea and from the river to the ends of the earth...May his name be forever. All the nations shall be blessed in him...Blessed be YHVH God, God of Israel, who alone does wonders" (Ps. 72).

The above has been misapplied to Jesus. The Psalm speaks of an earthly king. Jesus said his kingdom was not "of this world" (Jn. 18:36). Jesus did not achieve world peace. Nor does this Psalm support the Trinity, for how can God give justice and righteousness to his equal? It cannot be given to the "human" nature of the "god-man" because Jesus was not to attain kingship until after his resurrection! (Heb. 1:3; 2:9; 10:122; Ac. 2:33; 5:31; Eph. 1:20). As for the king seemingly living forever, this is oriental hyperbole: Cf. 1 Ki. 1:31, "May my lord King David live forever!" Cf. also Gen. 43:9; Exod. 21:6; Deut. 15:17; 18:5; 1 Sam. 1:22; 2 Sam. 7:13,16,19. Psalm 72 upholds the oneness and uncompromising singularity of God, "who *alone* does wonders."

"THE STONE WHICH THE BUILDERS REJECTED..."

Ps. 118:22: "The stone which the builders rejected has become the head of the corner." Christological interpretation: Messiah Jesus, the "stone," is rejected by his own people—the "builders"—and becomes the "head of all principality and power" (Col. 2:10; Eph. 1:20, 21; I Pet. 3:22). This interpretation presumes

Messiah's rejection by his own. When the birth of Jesus was announced, there was no hint of his rejection: "He will save his people from their sins" (Mt. 1:21). "The Lord God will give him the throne of his father David and he will reign over the house of Jacob forever; and of his kingdom there will be no end" (Lu. 1:32,33). Mary exulted: "He has helped his servant Israel, in remembrance of his mercy, as he spoke to our fathers, to Abraham and his posterity forever" (Lu. 1:54,55). Of John the Baptist, Jesus' forerunner, it was prophesied: "He will turn many of the sons of Israel to the Lord their God...the hearts of the fathers to the children to make ready for the Lord a people prepared" (Lu. 1:16,17). In all the birth-announcements concerning Jesus, there is no hint of failure. He was to be the ruler and redeemer of Israel.

At Messiah's coming, Israel is victorious: "Happy are you, O Israel! Who is like you, a people saved by YHVH, the shield of your help, and the sword of your triumph! Your enemies shall come fawning to you; and you shall tread upon their high places" (Deut. 33:29). "It shall come to pass in the latter days that the mountain of the house of YHVH shall be established as the highest of the mountains, and shall be raised above the hills; and all the nations shall flow to it, and many peoples shall come, and say: 'Come, let us go up to the mountain of YHVH, to the house of the God of Jacob; that he may teach us his ways and that we may walk in his paths.' For out of Zion shall go forth the law, and the word of YHVH from Jerusalem" (Isa. 2:2–4). "Many peoples and strong nations shall come to seek YHVH of hosts in Jerusalem, and to entreat the favor of YHVH...In those days ten men from the nations of every tongue shall take hold of the robe of a Jew, saying, 'Let us go with you, for we have heard that God is with you'" (Zech. 8:20–23). The notion that Messiah fails in his mission to save Israel, only to achieve it at a "second coming," is not found in Scripture.

The Christological interpretation of Ps. 118:22 is forced and ignores the context: V.23, "This is YHVH's doing; it is marvelous in our eyes": This is a joyous, not grievous, event for Israel.' According to vv. 2-4, Israel is not in disfavor. God gives Israel victory (v. 15). V. 18, "YHVH has chastened me sorely but has not given me over to death": This certainly is not a reference to Jesus.

Psalm 118 is a victory hymn, like the song of Moses (Exod. 15), and may have been sung at the rededication of the Temple, after the return of the Jews from the Babylonian Exile (Ezra 6:15 ff.) Or, perhaps it was a liturgical pageant, re-enacted annually by the Levitical Priests on the festivals of Passover and Tabernacles, and chanted chorally in a glorious procession to the gates of Jerusalem and the Temple Mount. Every Israelite could sing this Psalm of consolation—not for himself only but for the nation collectively: "Let *Israel* say, 'His lovingkindness endures forever'" (v. 2). "All nations surrounded me" (v. 10), though couched in the first person singular, obviously refers to the nation collectively (cf. V. 24). In metaphors, every word need not be pressed for symbolism. The key symbolic words in Ps. 118:22 are, "stone, rejected, corner." The metaphor would still hold if it were paraphrased: "The stone which was rejected has become the head of the corner."

The "rejected stone" is Israel, which suffered humiliating defeat from its neighboring nations, only to be triumphantly restored to its homeland: "The sons of those who oppressed you shall come bending low to you; and all who despised you shall bow down at your feet; they shall call you the City of YHVH, the Zion of the Holy One of Israel. Whereas you have been forsaken and hated, with no one passing through, I will make you majestic forever, a joy from age to age" (Isa. 60:14,15). "Thus says YHVH, the Redeemer of Israel and his Holy One, to one deeply despised, abhorred by the nations, the servant of rulers: Kings shall see and arise; princes, and they shall prostrate themselves; because of YHVH, who is faithful, the Holy One of Israel, who has chosen you" (Isa. 49:7; also 54:4; 62:4,5; 41:14; Ps. 44:13,23). The "builders" of v. 22 are ancient Israel's hostile neighbors, who held Israel in low esteem. Becoming the "head of the corner" signifies Israel's triumph over her enemies and exaltation "above the mountains" as a leader among nations (Isa. 2:2).

"A STONE OF OFFENSE"

Isa. 8:13-15,19-20: "YHVH of hosts, him shall you regard as holy; let him be your fear and let him be your dread. And he will become a sanctuary, a stone of offense and a rock of stumbling to both houses of Israel...And when they say to you, 'Consult the mediums and the wizards who chirp and mutter,' should not a people consult their God? Should they consult the dead on behalf of the living? To the Torah and to the testimony! If they do not speak according to this word, they have no light."

In I Pet. 2:8, Isaiah's "stone of offense" becomes Jesus. This interpretation is wrong. As the context indicates, the "stone" is YHVH of hosts, not Messiah. The deification of Jesus is the very sin of idolatry against which Isaiah is preaching! "YHVH of hosts, *him* shall you regard as holy; let *him* be your fear..." To deify mortal man, as Christianity has done, is to "consult the dead on behalf of the living [God]." The test is the "Torah and the testimony," whose unmistakable message is—ONE GOD! For those who remain faithful to the living God and shun idolatry, God will be a "sanctuary"—a source of confidence and strength (Isa. 4:5,f.; Ps. 27:5; 31:21; Prov. 18:10). The worship of *one* God will be difficult for the masses—a "stumblingstone"—for the temptation to idolatry is great (Nu. 15:39). Witness the relapse into idolatry of Israel at Sinai, so soon after God had demonstrated his saving power (Exod. 32; Ps. 106).

How is God a stumblingstone" to those who resort to idolatry? He permits their enemies to oppress them, testing their allegiance. Chastened, some return; others stumble and deny God (Judg. 2:11–23; 10:6–16). God is jealous for his exclusive worship. He does not brook any rivals, any "trinitarian" deities: "They have stirred me to jealousy with a non-god;...I will provoke them to jealousy with a foolish nation..." (Deut. 32:21).

"A PRECIOUS CORNER STONE"

Isa. 28:16: "Therefore thus says the Lord YHVH, 'Behold, I lay in Zion for a precious corner stone, a sure foundation: he that believes shall not make haste.'" The Christian Scriptures apply this to Jesus (Rom. 9:32, 33; I Pet. 2:4–6). The new JPS translation renders Isa. 28:16: "Assuredly, thus said the Lord GOD: 'Behold, I will found in Zion, stone by stone, *a tower of precious cornerstones,* exceedingly firm; he who trusts need not fear." (The italicized words are footnoted—"Meaning of Heb. uncertain.") David compares God to a "high tower," and a "tower of strength," Ps. 18:2; 61:3; 144:2. Proverbs 18:10 says: "The name of YHVH is a strong tower; the righteous run into it and are safe." YHVH is the "tower of precious cornerstones," which offers protection to those who trust in him (cf. vv. 5,6). It is YHVH of hosts who saves his people, as the concluding verse 29 affirms.

If Isa. 28:16 is pressed as messianic, we would point out that after the founding in Zion of the stone, God says: "I will make justice the line, and righteousness the plummet" (v. 17). Justice and righteousness were not established in the earth pursuant to Jesus' coming.

"YHVH SAID TO MY LORD"

Ps. 110:1: "YHVH said to my lord: 'sit at my right hand till I make your enemies your footstool.'" Christian interpreters refer this to Jesus' ascension to heaven and being seated at God's right hand. (Mt. 22:44; Mk. 12:36; Lu. 20:42,43; Acts 2:34; I Cor. 15:25; Heb. 1:13). "Messianic Jews" hold to the trinitarian belief that Jesus and YHVH are one and the same. But interpreting the above as "God said to Jesus," contradicts this.

Psalm 110 was written for the priestly choirmaster (Ps. 109:1). The Levites, not David, sang the Psalms in the Temple (I Chron. 16:4–7; Ezra 3:10,11). Thus, when a Levite or Israelite chanted the words "YHVH said to my lord," the second "lord" referred to King David." It has no Christological overtones, as though a divine being were seated in heaven at the literal right-hand of God. The right-hand position denotes favor (I Ki. 2:19; Ps. 80:17; 45:9). The meaning is that

God invests the king with divine ruling authority, Ps. 45:6,7; I Chron. 29:23; cf. Num. 36:2,10; I Ki. 1:31.

Alternative interpretation: The Psalm was written *for* King David—*mizmor l'David*. Thus, the unnamed Psalmist is speaking respectfully of "his lord" King David, as in I Ki. 1:31, "May my lord King David live forever!" Cf. Nu. 36:2: "YHVH commanded my lord." Here Moses is meant, as indicated by v. 10.

"YHVH CREATED ME AT THE BEGINNING"

Proverbs 8:22–36: "YHVH possessed me in the beginning of his way, before his works of old. From everlasting was I fashioned, at the beginning, from the origin of the earth." Christian interpreters relate this to Jn. 1:1: "In the beginning was the Word and the Word was with God and the Word was God." The subject of Proverbs 8, however, is wisdom not the Messiah. Wisdom is *created*. God alone is eternal; nothing is co-eternal" with him. There is no co-creator" (Col. 1:16); God is the sole Creator: "I am YHVH who made all things, who stretched out the heavens alone, who spread out the earth—Who was with me?" (Isa. 44:24; cf. Ps. 33:6). Wisdom is not a supernatural being.

"UNTO US A CHILD IS BORN"

Isa. 9:6,7: "For a child has been born to us, a son has been given us. And the government shall be upon his shoulder, and his name shall be called 'Wonderful, Counselor, Mighty God, Everlasting Father, Prince of Peace.' Of the increase of the government and of peace there is no end, on the throne of David, and on his kingdom, to establish it and uphold it with justice and with righteousness from now and forevermore. The zeal of YHVH of hosts will do this." This does not fit the Christian messiah: The child is a scion of King David (cf. Ps. 132:11,12) and is given to *Israel* as ruler. He is not rejected by his people to become ruler of the Gentiles but initiates an *enduring* kingdom of peace (cf. Mt. 21:43; Ac. 18:6). Jesus' descent from David is questionable, the genealogy being invalid. (See our discussion under "Jesus.") According to Paul, "there is one God, the Father, and one lord, Jesus Christ" (I Cor. 8:6). The "Mighty God" is YHVH, and He alone (Isa. 10:20,21; Deut. 10:17; Jer. 32:18; Neh. 9:32; Ps. 24:8, etc). No man may be designated "God" (Hos. 11:9). While it is true that David's heir Eliakim is to be "a father to the inhabitants of Jerusalem and to the house of Judah" (Isa. 22:21), it is not in the Christological sense of "life-giver." Jesus himself implied that there is "one Father," who is in heaven (Mt. 6:9) Jesus cannot be said to be "everlasting": He was *created*; he is "the *first-born* of all creation" (Col. 1:15; Heb. 1:5, 6; Rev. 3:14). As for calling a king "everlasting," cf. "May my lord

King David live forever!" (I Ki. 1:31; Neh. 2:3). The meaning is, May he never lack ruling descendants (II Sam. 7:16; Jer. 33:17).

There is another problem for trinitarians: How can Jesus be "mighty god" and "prince of peace" simultaneously? Trinitarian answer: "As a man he was prince of peace but at his resurrection he was restored to godship." Our reply: Why, then, is "prince of peace" mentioned last?

Some translators render Isaiah 9:6: "Wonderful Counselor of the Mighty God, of the everlasting Father, the Prince of Peace"; or, "Wonderful in counsel is the Mighty God, etc." (cf. Isa. 28:29.) The Hebrew warrants this. Others leave the names of the child untranslated: *Peleh Yoetz El-Gibbor Avi-ad Sar-Shalom.* This conforms to Biblical Hebrew's habit of joining God's name to persons and places to connote aspiration, gratitude, or prophecy. Jacob named the place where he had wrestled with the angel, *Peni-El,* "The Face of God" (Gen. 32:30); the altar at Shechem, *El-Elohe-Yisrael,* "God, the God of Israel" (Gen. 33:20); and the altar at Luz, *El-Bethel,* "The God of Bethel" (Gen. 35:7). Moses built an altar after the defeat of Amalek and named it *YHVH-Nisi,* "YHVH My Banner" (Exod. 17:15). Jerusalem was called *YHVH-Tsidkenu,* "YHVH Our Righteousness" (Jer. 33:15,16), and *YHVH-Shama,* "YHVH is there" (Ezek. 48:35). Israel was called *YHVH-Tsidkenu,* YHVH Our Righteousness (Jer. 23:6). Cf. also Jer. 14:9; Dan. 9:19. Other Biblical names joined to God's name are, *Michael,* "Who is like God?"; *Shmuel,* "Heard of God"; *Eliezer,* "God is my Help," etc.

When God's name is joined to the ruler's, it signifies that he rules by God's authority: "He shall stand and feed his flock in the strength of YHVH, in *the majesty* of the *name of YHVH his God*" (Mic. 5:4).

Was Jesus truly a "prince of peace" (cf. Mt. 10:34)? He did not establish his kingdom of peace *immediately,* as Isaiah prophesied (cf. Ac. 1:6,7; Heb. 10:12,13; 1 Thess. 5:1)! Jesus said his kingdom was not earthly, in effect denying he was "king of the Jews" (Jn. 18:33-36). A kingdom of "justice and judgment," by definition, is an *earthly* kingdom—heaven has no need of "justice" (Mt. 6:10; Job 25:2; Ps. 103:20)! Messiah's kingdom is earthly, peaceful and just. His reign commences immediately—"from *now* and forevermore." "He will not fail or be discouraged until he has established justice in the earth" (Isa. 42:4). Jesus did not fulfill this. There is no hint in the Isaiah passage that the government of righteousness must await a "second coming" of Messiah. The everlasting nature of the Davidic kingdom does not imply supernaturalness. David was promised an "everlasting" kingdom, 1 Ki. 1:31; 2 Chron. 13:5; Ps. 8:50; 89:3,4,29; 132:10-18.

To force a trinitarian meaning upon Isa. 9:6,7 is contrary to the spirit of Monotheism, so pervasive throughout Scripture.

"A SHOOT…FROM THE STUMP OF JESSE"

Isa. 11:1-9: "There shall come forth a shoot from the stump of Jesse…his delight shall be in the fear of YHVH…The wolf shall dwell with the lamb…They shall not hurt nor destroy in all My holy mountain for the earth shall be full of the knowledge of YHVH…." Isaiah's prophecy does not point to Jesus nor support the Trinity: David's descendant "fears YHVH"—no trinitarian co-equality! He is not supernatural. He establishes universal peace and ends all violence. The knowledge of God fills the earth. Jesus did not bring this about. Nor is there any suggestion of a "second" coming.

"MY SERVANT DAVID SHALL FEED THEM"

Ezek. 34:23,24: "I will set over them one shepherd, my servant David, and he shall feed them…And I, YHVH, will be their God, and my servant David shall be prince among them." Messiah is God's *servant*, not equal (cf. 37:25). *YHVH* is God; Messiah David is *prince*. Messiah rules *among* his people—on *earth*, not in heaven.

"RULER IN ISRAEL"

Micah 5:2,4: "And you, Bethlehem Ephrathah, least among the thousands of Judah—from you shall go forth for me one that shall be ruler in Israel—whose origin is from old, from ancient days…He shall stand and shepherd by the strength of YHVH, by the power of the name of YHVH his God."

Micah's prophecy is applied to Jesus, Mt. 2:6; Jn. 7:42. This, however, is a misinterpretation: There is no valid genealogy tracing Jesus' descent from Judah. Regarding Jesus being "ruler in Israel"—when Pilate asked him if he was king of the Jews, he replied: "You have said so." Then Pilate told the Jews, "I find no crime in this man, implying that he was not guilty of sedition for he made no claim to royalty (Mt. 27:11 ff.; Lu. 23:2-4; Jn. 18:34-36).

The expression "from ancient days" (*miyme-kedem*) is identical to that used in Mic. 7:20: "You will give truth to Jacob, steadfast love to Abraham, which you swore to our fathers from *days of old* (*miyme-kedem).*" (Cf. also 2 Ki. 19:25; Isa. 19:11; 37:26; 51:9; Mal. 3:4 and note the use of a similar expression for human kings.) Messiah's roots hark back to ancient times—to the patriarchs Abraham and Jacob, to whom the promise of a future deliverer was first made. "Whose goings forth"—*motsaotav*, from *yatsa*, is never used of the infinite, eternal God—Isa. 40:28. Cf. Nu. 34:8; Josh. 15:4,11.

"He shall feed his flock in the name of YHVH *his* God." (Cf. Jn. 15:16; 14:13,14; 16:23.) Messiah is not God but is subject *to* God!

Attempting to prove the "eternality" of the second person of the Trinity from Micah 5:2 is futile. Messiah is God's *servant*; he does not rule by his *own* authority but by the *strength of YHVH*. He is subject to God: "His delight shall be in the *fear* of God" (Isa. 11:3).

"WHOM THEY HAVE PIERCED"

Zech. 12:10, "And I will pour out upon the house of David and upon the inhabitants of Jerusalem a spirit of mercy and supplication and they shall look to me [*elai*] whom they have pierced. And they shall mourn for it [*alav*=Jerusalem] as one mourns for an only child and shall feel bitterness for it as one feels bitterness for a first-born." Christian interpretation: In the end-time, God will move the Jews to repentance and they shall mourn for their Messiah whom they have rejected (Jn. 19:34-37).

The above interpretation is flawed: Zechariah 12:10 is not "messianic" but concerns God's deliverance of Jerusalem. It is not a prophecy for the "end-time" but for the *immediate* future, as indicated by *hineh*, literally "here" (v. 2). Cf. Gen. 18:9; 19:8, etc.

God is moved to compassion for his rebellious people: "Return to me…and I will return to you…YHVH will again comfort Zion and again choose Jerusalem" (Zech. 1:3,16,17; cf. 8:3; 10:6). God's compassionate returning to his people is a recurrent theme in the prophets: "Neither will I hide my face any more from them, for I have *poured out* my *spirit upon the house of Israel*" (Ezek. 39:29; cf. Exod. 3:7; Dan. 9:18).

The traditional translation of Zech. 12:10, "They shall look *upon* him," does not conform to the Hebrew. The correct understanding is, "They shall look to me *(elai)*"—They shall again acknowledge me (cf. Isa 51:1,2), whom they have pierced"—provoked by neglecting my law: "Sons have I reared and. brought up but they have rebelled against me" (Isa. 1:2; 65:2,3; 37:23).

"THE SON OF MAN"

In Daniel, chapter 7, in a night vision, Daniel beholds one like a son of man [*bar-enosh*=.'human being'] who is presented to the "Ancient of Days," and granted an everlasting kingdom. The Christian interpretation is that the "son of man" is Jesus. Daniel's man-like being is not the son of God but *a* "son of man," a human being, who receives a kingdom from the "Ancient of Days." He is neither co-equal nor co-eternal with the "Ancient of Days" who pre-exists him. The "Ancient of Days" is served by a myriad of heavenly creatures, whereas the "son of Man" is served by the "nations." Only one "Most High" is mentioned (v. 25). The "saints of the Most High" are more prominent than the "son of man." He is mentioned once whereas they are mentioned four times and receive more authority than he. Trinitarians must answer: Did Jesus retain his humanity in heaven? If yes, his "body" was not sacrificed(Heb. 10:~ I Cor 15:44; cf. 47). Clearly, Daniel's "son of man" is not the trinitarian, incarnate deity of Christian theology.

"MELCHIZEDEK...PRIEST OF GOD MOST HIGH"

Gen. 14:18-20: "And Melchizedek king of Salem...was priest of God Most High." Cf. Heb. 7:3, "He [Melchizedek] is without father or mother or genealogy, and has neither beginning of days nor end of life, but resembling the son of God continues a priest forever." Problems: As "priest of *God most high*," he cannot typify the "second, co-equal person" of the Trinity! Also, Jesus had a father, a mother and a genealogy!

"I SAW THE LORD..."'

Isa. 6:1, ff. : "In the year King Uzziah died I saw the Lord sitting upon a throne...my eyes have seen the King, YHVH of hosts!": Isaiah saw no "tri-une god"!

MESSIANIC ERA A TIME OF FAVOR FOR ISRAEL

Messiah was not to be rejected by Israel: "In his days Judah will be saved and Israel shall dwell securely" (Jer. 23:6). "Your people shall be willing in the day of your power" (Ps. 110:3). Messiah is heralded by Elijah, who is *desired* of Israel: "Behold, I send my messenger to prepare the way before me...the messenger of the covenant *whom you desire*...he will purify the sons of Levi...Then the offering of Judah and Jerusalem will be pleasing to YHVH as in the days of old and as in former years" (Mal. 3:1-4). Messiah's coming is a time of restoration, not alienation, for the Jewish people: "He will turn the hearts of the fathers to their children and the hearts of the children to their fathers...(Mal. 4:6). Messiah rules on the "throne of David" (Jer. 23:5; Ezek. 37:24; Hos. 3:5), implying a peaceful rule with willing Jewish subjects. The servant of Isaiah 53 is rejected of "*men,*" not Israel.

JEWS STILL AWAIT MESSIAH

A messianic tract invites its readers to examine the prophecies concerning Messiah and concludes: "If Jesus did not fulfill the prophecies, we Jews should reject him!" THIS IS PRECISELY WHY JEWS STILL *AWAIT* THE MESSIAH! Deut. 18:22.

*　　　　　　*　　　　　　*

(NOTE TO READER: Obviously, we have not covered *every* "messianic" reference used by Christian missionaries but we do offer the following guidelines for interpretation: No scriptural reference should be interpreted apart from its *context*. Carefully consider the *context* and, if possible, the Hebrew original, and you will arrive at a correct understanding.)

CHAPTER 9

THE SUFFERING SERVANT
(ISA. 52:13–53:12)

Of all the "proof-texts" cited to substantiate the claims made for Jesus, Isaiah 53 probably is the most oft-quoted. According to Bible scholars, however, the text in many places is obscure and problemtical for translators.

The passages missionaries emphasize are: "He was despised and rejected…He has borne our griefs…He was wounded for our transgressions…He bore the sin of many and made intercession for the transgressors."

If Isaiah 53 is applied to the Christian messiah, it poses problems: The "suffering servant" is a man, not a deity; and there is no mention of any pre-human existence, resurrection, kingship, or kingdom—aspects of the Christian messiah.

ISRAEL PERSONIFIED

In the prophets, Israel, Jerusalem, and Zion are synonymous, and are frequently *personified*: "Awake, awake, put on your strength, O Zion; put on your beautiful garments, O Jerusalem, the holy city; for there shall no more come into you the uncircumcised and the unclean. Shake yourself from the dust, arise, O captive Jerusalem; loose the bonds from your neck, O captive daughter of Zion…Behold, my servant shall prosper, he shall be exalted and lifted up, and shall be very high. As many as were astonished at him—his appearance was so marred, beyond human semblance, and his form beyond that of the sons of men—so shall he startle many nations; kings shall shut their mouths because of him; for that which has not been told them they shall see, and that which they have not heard they shall understand. Who has believed what we have heard? And to whom has the arm of YHVH been revealed?" (Isa. 52:1,2,13–15; 53:1).

THE "SERVANT" ISRAEL

The "servant" is Israel: "But you, Israel, my servant, Jacob, whom I have chosen..." (Isa. 41:8,9; 43:10; 44:1, 2,21,26; 45:4;49:3; Jer. 46:27; Ps. 136:22). The servant's incredible disfigurement is a metaphor for the plight of Israel and Jerusalem during the Babylonian captivity (Isa. 51:19,20).

ISRAEL'S HUMBLE BEGINNINGS LIKE A DESERT PLANT

What "startles the nations" is the restoration of Israel and Jerusalem (52:8–10; cf. Exod. 15:14-16). The report is "incredible" because of Israel's seeming impotence and insignificance: "For he grew up before him like a young plant, and like a root out of dry ground" (cf. Isa. 27:6; Exod. 15:17). Israel's humble beginnings are compared to a "tender plant" in arid ground: "He found him in a desert land, and in the howling waste of the wilderness; he compassed him about, he cared for him, he kept him as the apple of his eye" (Deut. 32:10). "As for your birth, on the day your were born your navel string was not cut, nor were you washed with water to cleanse you, nor rubbed with salt, nor swathed with bands. No eye pitied you, to do any of these things to you out of compassion for you; but you were cast out on the open field, for you were abhorred on the day you were born. And when I passed by you, and saw you weltering in your blood, I said to you in your blood, 'Live, and grow up like a plant of the field'" (Ezek. 16:4-7; 19:10-14). "You brought a vine out of Egypt; you drove out the nations and planted it. You cleared the ground for it; it took deep root and filled the land" (Ps. 80:8,9). Israel's numbers were meager compared to her populous neighbors: "You were the fewest of all peoples" (Deut. 7:7; I Chron. 16:19). It is incredible that God should have chosen this impotent people, which at first was like a dormant, unpromising root in dry ground! Who would have predicted that this downtrodden and exiled people would be so gloriously restored to its homeland!

"DESPISED AND REJECTED"

"He had no form or comeliness that we should look at him, nor beauty that we should desire him. He was despised and forsaken of men; a man of sorrows and acquainted with disease; and as one from whom men hide their faces, he was despised and we esteemed him not." This is oppressed and exiled Israel: "You have made us a reproach to our neighbors, a scoffing and a derision to them that are round about us. You have made us a byword among the nations, a shaking of the head among the peoples" (Ps. 44:13-16). "All your lovers have forgotten you; they care nothing for you" (Jer. 30:14). "I will make you a desolation and an object of reproach among the nations round about you and in the sight of all who pass by" (Ezek. 5:14–17). "Fear not, you worm Jacob, you men of Israel!" (Isa. 41:14). "This is a people robbed and plundered, they are all of them trapped in holes and hidden in prisons; they have become a prey with none to rescue, a spoil with none to say, 'Restore!'" (Isa. 42:22). "Thus says YHVH, the Redeemer of Israel and his Holy One, to one deeply despised, abhorred by the nations, the servant of rulers: 'Kings shall see and arise; princes, and they shall prostrate themselves; because of YHVH, who is faithful, the Holy One of Israel, who has chosen you'" (Isa. 49:7). "You will forget the shame of your youth, and the reproach of your widowhood you will remember no more" (Isa. 54:4). "You shall no more be termed Forsaken, and your land shall no more be termed Desolate…(Isa. 62:4).

JEWISH MESSIAH NOT UNLOVELY AND FORSAKEN

The Suffering Servant of Isaiah 53 is unlovely and forsaken. By contrast, the Jewish Messiah is "fairest of the sons of men" (Ps. 45:2; Isa. 52:7) and received by his own (Ps. 110:3). He is not "despised and rejected": "Him shall the nations seek" (Isa. 11:10).

As for the Christian messiah, where is there any hint that he "had no form or beauty"? Jesus was not "despised and rejected": "Great crowds followed him…" (Mt. 4:25). The Suffering Servant is "despised and rejected of *men*," *not* of Jews!

"A man of sorrows and acquainted with disease": An allusion to the sorrowful state of exiled Israel: "The whole head is sick, and the whole heart faint. From the sole of the foot even to the head, there is no soundness in it, but bruises and sores and bleeding wounds…Your country lies desolate, your cities are burned with fire; in your very presence aliens devour your land; it is desolate, as overthrown by aliens" (Isa. 1:5–7; 30:26). "Your hurt is incurable, and your wound is grievous…I will restore health to you, and your wounds will I heal, says YHVH, because they have called you an outcast: 'It is Zion, for whom no one cares!'" (Jer. 30:12-17). "All who pass along the way clap their hands at you; they hiss and wag their heads at the daughter of Jerusalem; 'Is this the city which was called the perfection of beauty, the joy of all the earth?'" (Lam. 2:15).

"He was wounded for our transgressions…by his stripes are we healed." (Cf. Isa. 30:26.) Neither the Jewish People nor the world have yet been "healed."

"Smitten of God and afflicted": "I smote him, I hid my face and was angry…but I will heal him" (Isa. 57:16; 42:24,25; Jer. 14:19; Hos. 6:1): Israel is punished by God but will be forgiven. (If Christians believe it was *God* who afflicted Jesus, the Jews should not be blamed.)

"Like a lamb led to the slaughter, and like a sheep that before its shearers is dumb, he opened not his mouth": Despite untold sufferings, Israel does not deny God or accuse him of injustice. Rather, it attributes its sufferings to its own way-wardness: "Nay, for your sake we are slain all the day long, and accounted as sheep for the slaughter . All this has come upon us, though we have not forgotten you, or been false to your covenant" (Ps. 44:11,22,17; cf. Job 1:11; 2:5,9,10). (Jesus was not uncomplaining [Mt. 27:46; Mk. 15:34]).

"By his knowledge shall the righteous one, my servant, make many to be accounted righteous." We must ask Christian interpreters: Who is the "righteous one, my servant"?

"He shall see seed, he shall prolong his days.": This refers to God's promise to the Patriarchs of a great progeny: "Their seed shall be known among the nations…all who see them shall acknowledge them, that they are a people whom YHVH has blessed" (Isa. 61:9). The Suffering Servant has physical descendants. How could this apply to the celibate Jesus? "*Long* life," not *eternal* life, is prom-ised! But Jesus is said to be "co-eternal" with the Father!

"He shall divide the spoil with the mighty": Israel's oppressors, like her ancient Egyptian enslavers, will contribute their wealth to Israel's prosperity: You shall eat the wealth of the nations…The abundance of the sea shall be turned to you…They shall bring gold and frankincense…You shall suck the milk of nations, you shall suck the breast of kings…" (Isa. 60:5-7; 61:6; Zeph. 2:9).

"He made intercession for the transgressors": Israel is the "messianic" people, which gives light to the nations and justice to the world: "Behold, my servant, whom I uphold…will not fail or be discouraged till he has established justice in the earth…I have given you as a covenant to the people, a light to the nations" (Isa. 42:1,4,6,7). "You are my servant, Israel, in whom I will be glorified…I will give you as a light to the nations, that my salvation may reach to the end of the earth" (Isa. 49:3,6).

*　　　　　*　　　　　*

The burden of Isaiah 53, like much of Isaiah and the other prophetic writings, is the plight of exiled Israel and its restoration to its homeland. The "suffering ser-vant" atones for the sins of *Israel,* whereas Jesus was to have atoned for the sins of *all* mankind (Jn. 1:29; 3:16). If Isaiah 53 is interpreted as referring to an individ-ual, it is a *man*, not a deity. There is no mention of kingship, a kingdom, or a res-urrection! Applying Isaiah 53 to the Christian messiah presents a problem for trinitarians: To speak of God's *servant* is inconsistent with the trinitarian concept that messiah-Jesus is God!

"THE WHOLE COUNSEL OF GOD"

Regarding the interpretation of Scripture, we have encountered the following position among "Messianic Jews": When there is a seeming contradiction in Scripture, the text in question must be "viewed in the light of the entire Bible." One should not focus on a few statements to the exclusion of other Biblical evidence. Two passages are quoted to support this approach: Deut 8:3, "...*every* word that proceeds from the mouth of God"; Acts 20:27, "I did not shrink from declaring to you the *whole* counsel of God."

We, for our part, have followed the above approach in our interpretation of Isaiah 53. As we interpret Scripture, we trust we will be accorded the same privilege to use the "comparative", interpretative method, as do the missionaries.

CHAPTER 10

"ORIGINAL SIN"

CHRISTIAN DOCTRINE OF "ORIGINAL SIN"

According to Christian doctrine, the first, or "original" sin was committed by father Adam and transmitted to his descendants, together with its death-penalty (Rom. 5:12): "And YHVH God commanded the man, saying, 'You may freely eat of every tree of the garden; but of the tree of the knowledge of good and evil you shall not eat, for in the day you eat of it you shall surely die'" (Gen. 2:16,17). Eve eats the forbidden fruit, shares it with Adam and is punished with painful childbearing. To Adam, God says: "Cursed is the ground because of you; in toil you shall eat of it all the days of your life...In the sweat of your face you shall eat bread till you return to the ground, for out of it you were taken; you are dust, and to dust you shall return'" (Gen. 3:17–19).

Continuing with Christian doctrine...The curse of sin and death is lifted through God's plan of "Salvation": "As by the offense of one, judgment came upon all men to condemnation; even so by the righteousness of one, the free gift came upon all men to justification of life" (Rom. 5:18,19; I Cor. 15:22; Mk. 10:45). When Adam sinned, he forfeited perfect human life and immortality for himself and his descendants. To remove the curse of sin and death and satisfy "divine justice," another perfect human had to be sacrificed. Since imperfect, sinful man could not provide the redemptive price, God provided it in Jesus, the "perfect man." This is called the "Ransom Sacrifice."

"RANSOM SACRIFICE" BASED ON A FALSE PREMISE

The "Ransom Sacrifice" falsely assumes that man was created to live forever. Man, created from the dust (*Adam* is akin to *adamah*, 'earth'), became a "living soul"—not an "immortal" soul (Gen. 2:7). Being created from the dust implies mortality, perishability. What comes from the earth must eventually decompose and revert to its essential elements: Gen. 3:19; 18:27; Job 4:19; Ps. 10:18; 78:39; 89:48; 90:3; 103:14; Eccl. 3:19-21; 9:5; 12:7; Ps. 49:7-9; Isa. 40:6; I Cor. 15:47. Mortality is man's natural and intended state (cf. Rom. 1:23; I Cor. 15:53; Heb. 9:27); it is not due to Eden's transgression.

IN "GOD' S IMAGE"—BUT NOT A GOD

Being created in "God's image" does not imply perfection or immortality. A "perfect" man could not be tempted (cf. Heb. 4:15). *After* the transgression in Eden, mortal, sin-prone man is still in "God's image" (Gen. 9:6)! The penalty for eating the forbidden fruit was not mortality—or the loss of immortality—but *premature* death. Eve was not sentenced to "mortality"—she already was mortal. Her sentence was painful childbirth and submission to her husband.

Paul's teaching that death is due to "original sin" (Rom. 5:12) is contradicted by the words, "Let me die the death of the righteous [by not dying prematurely]" (Num. 23:10; Isa. 65:20). According to Ps. 90:10, an average life-span is 70–80 years. Righteous Job lived 140 years and "died, an old man, and full of days" (Job 42:16,17; cf. 5:26; Gen. 25:8; 35:29). Death is not necessarily due to sin ; the "righteous" die as well.

"IN THE DAY YOU EAT OF IT"

God warned Adam: "In *the day* you eat of it you shall surely die" (Gen. 2:17). "In the day" is a Hebrew idiom for "when": "These are the generations of the heavens and the earth *when* they were created, *in the day* YHVH God made the earth and the heavens" (Gen. 2:4). More than "one day" was occupied in their creation! God was telling Adam, "*When* you eat of it you shall surely die." But Adam lived 930 years (Gen. 5:5)! God mercifully rescinded his decree, as evidenced by his provision of skin-garments for Adam and Eve (Gen. 3:21). God is not implacable (Ps. 86:15). After the Flood, God vowed never again to bring universal destruction (Gen. 8:21,22). Similarly, God was prepared to avert his decree against Sodom and Gomorrah (Gen. ch. 18). At the intercession of Moses, God rescinded his decree against Israel (Exod. 32:11–14). Gen. 5:1-5, a capsule of Adam's life, takes no account of the transgression in the Garden of Eden.

NO "UNIVERSAL" GUILT

The Eden story contains no hint of transmission of guilt to the human race. Scripture rejects collective guilt (Ezek. ch. 18). After Eden, Adam still may choose between good and evil (Gen. 3:22). Cain's sin is not attributed to his father Adam; he is a free moral agent: "If you do well, will you not be accepted? And if you do not do well, sin is couching at the door; its desire is for you, but you can master it" (Gen. 4:7; cf. Deut. 30:19; Ps. 119:133). Enoch mastered sin, was not burdened with "Adamic guilt" and "walked with God" (Gen. 5:24). Noah the "righteous" does not inherit "Adamic sin" and has an intimate relationship with God who covenants with him (Gen. 6:9; 9:9-17). After the flood, Noah presents a pleasing offering to God, who declares: "I will never again curse the ground because of man, for the imagination of man's heart is evil from his youth…" (Gen. 8:21). God does not attribute human sinfulness to Adam; man's evil inclination is natural. Moses rejects "collective guilt": "If one man sins, will you be angry with the entire community?" (Num. 16:22).

JESUS NOT ADAM'S EQUIVALENT

The sacrifice of Jesus was supposed to satisfy "divine justice"—"a life for a life" (Exod. 21:23; Deut. 19:21). He was to be a ransom for the "perfect life" Adam forfeited (I Cor. 15:45). But Jesus was not the equivalent of Adam! Adam was created a mortal human whereas Jesus allegedly had a pre-human, heavenly existence, was incarnated as a human (I Cor. 15:47; 2:8; Jn. 1:1,14; 8:58; 17:5) and was "sinless." He was not, therefore, "like his brothers in every respect" (Heb. 2:17); he was *more* than man.

Jesus provides "eternal, heavenly life" (I Cor. 15:51–54; Php. 3:20,21). But such was not lost by Adam; he did not have it in the first place. Nor did Jesus remove painful childbirth, male dominance of the woman (I Tim. 2:12), a cursed earth, and human toil!

EVE, NOT ADAM, SINNED FIRST

Paul blames Adam for introducing sin into the world (Rom. 5:12,14; I Cor. 15:21); but Eve sinned first (Gen. 3:6)!

FORGIVENESS OF SIN

In Christian theology Jesus provides forgiveness of sin and salvation (Mt. 26:28; Col. 1:14, etc.). But forgiveness of sin and salvation were available *before* Jesus: "Blessed is he whose transgression is forgiven, whose sin is covered. Blessed is the man to whom YHVH does not impute iniquity He does not deal with us according to our sins, nor requite us according to our iniquities" (Ps. 32:1,2,5; 103:3,10,13). "If the wicked man turns away from all his sins…he shall surely live…None of the transgressions which he has committed shall be remembered against him. By the righteousness which he has done he shall live" (Ezek. 18:21,22). "I will heal their faithlessness; I will love them freely…" (Hos. 14:4) [They are "freely" forgiven, *without* a "ransom."] See also II Sam. 12:13; 22:21-24; Job 33:26–28; Prov. 28:13; Ps. 78:38,39; 30:3,4; Isa. 1:18; 43:25; 44:22; 55:7; Jer. 17:14; 31:34; 33:8; Mic. 7:18,19.

"WASH YOURSELVES; MAKE YOURSELVES CLEAN"

The freedom to choose between good and evil was available *before* Jesus: "If you do well, will you not be accepted? And if you do not do well, sin is couching at the door; its desire is for you. But *you shall master it*" (Gen. 4:7; Deut. 30:19). "Wash yourselves; make yourselves clean; remove the evil of your doings from before my eyes…though your sins be as scarlet, they shall be as white as snow; though they be red like crimson, they shall be as wool" (Isa. l:16–18). "Let the wicked forsake his way, and the unrighteous man his thoughts; let him return to YHVH, that he may have mercy on him, and to our God, for he will abundantly pardon" (Isa. 55:6,7; Ezek. 33:10,11).

Whereas in Christianity, sinning is inevitable, we find a contrary view in Hebrew Scripture: "A soul *that sins unwittingly*…the priest shall make atonement for them and they shall be forgiven" (Lev. 4:2,13,20,22; Numb. 15:25,26). Sin offerings are brought *if* and *when* one sinned.

Despite the universality of evil, Noah, Abraham and others are declared righteous (Gen. 6:5,8,9; 15:6; Rom. 4:3; Gal. 3:6; Jas. 2:23). Therefore Paul is not correct in saying "none is righteous" (Rom. 3:10)!

THE "EVIL AND GOOD INCLINATIONS"

We are created with a "good inclination" and an "evil inclination." This should not seem strange since everything in creation is attributed to God: "I make peace and create evil; I, YHVH, do all these things" (Isa. 45:7; cf. Deut. 32:39). The "evil inclination" is innate; it is not due to Adam's transgression (Gen. 8:20,21; Ps. 103:13,14). The "good inclination" can overcome the "evil inclination" (Gen. 4:7; Ps. 119:133). We were made "a little lower than God and crowned with glory and honor" (Ps. 8:5). This is not mankind in a "pre-sin" state but is an ongoing condition! The Psalmist takes no account of the "Eden transgression" and Jesus never mentions the "Fall of Adam." Hebrew Scripture does not present a "depraved, sin-laden" man.

CHRISTIAN "PROOF TEXTS" FOR "ORIGINAL SIN" SHOW ONLY THAT HUMAN SINFULNESS IS INNATE, NOT DUE TO A "PRIMAL TRANSGRESSION"

Gen. 6:5: "YHVH saw that the wickedness of man was great in the earth, and that every imagination of the thoughts of his heart was only evil continually." This is not a *universal* indictment because Noah is "righteous" (vv. 8,9). The *generation of Noah* is condemned, not humankind. If *one man* is righteous, *all* of Adam's descendants are not inherently evil.

Paul says: "None is righteous, no, not one" (Rom. 3:10). Paul is quoting Ps. 14:1-3 and 53:1-3: "They have all gone astray, they are all alike corrupt; there is none that does good, no, not one." This is not an indictment of the *human race* but of those who "deny God" and "eat up my people" (vv. 1,4). The Psalmist is using hyperbole and does not mean literally that there is not a single good person. Compare Gen. 6:5,8,9, where, despite the universality of evil, Noah is declared righteous.

Gen. 8:20,21: "When YHVH smelled the pleasing odor [of Noah's sacrifice], YHVH said in his heart, 'I will never again curse the ground because of man, for the *imagination of man's heart* is evil from his youth'" "Imagination," Heb. *yetzer*, is from a root meaning "create" and could be translated "natural impulse." The impulse to sin is innate, not due to "Adam's transgression." God will never again curse the ground because of man because the "evil inclination" is innate. But sin can be overcome: "Sin lies at the door and its desire is for you. But *you shall master it*" (Gen. 4:7). David prays: "Keep back your servant from presumptuous sins; *let them not rule me*. Then shall I be upright and I shall be innocent from great transgression" (Ps. 19:13; 119:133). David does not seek deliverance from *all* sin but prays for mastery over "presumptuous" and "great" sins. Righteousness requires only a *preponderance* of good deeds (Aboth 3:19). Job prayed: "Let me be weighed in a *just scale* that God may know my integrity" (Job 31:6). Job is asking God to temper justice with mercy, in consideration of his human frailties and limitations. Rabbi Joshua ben Perachyah taught: "Judge every man in the scale of merit" (Mishna, Aboth 1:6). Just as we are to judge others with the scale weighted in their favor, we ask God to consider our *merits* as against our *sins*.

I Ki. 8:46; II Chron. 6:36–40: "If they sin against you—for there is no one who does not sin...if they repent forgive your people." Human sinfulness is innate, not attributable to Adam. Repentance brings forgiveness.

Ps. 51:l—17: "Have mercy upon me, O God...blot out my transgressions. Wash me thoroughly from my iniquity, and cleanse me from my sin!...Behold, I was brought forth in iniquity, and in sin did my mother conceive me...Hide your face from my sins, and blot out all my iniquities. Create in me a clean heart, O God...Restore to me the joy of your salvation...Deliver me from bloodguiltiness,

O God…You have no delight in sacrifice…The sacrifice acceptable to God is a broken spirit; a broken and a contrite heart, O God, you will not despise." David's statement of being "conceived in sin and iniquity," is not a reference to *all* human birth, as though all are born in sin. David is not talking about sin as a "state" but as an individual *act*. There is no record of David's birth. Perhaps Scripture discreetly avoids mention of it so as not to cast a cloud upon Israel's illustrious king. Rather than being perpetually in bondage to "original sin," having to await "Christian redemption," David prays for cleansing and forgiveness. David's melancholy expression stems from a deeply penitential mood. This same David who said, "In sin did my mother conceive me," also said, "Judge me, O YHVH, according to my righteousness" (Ps. 7:8; cf. 18:20,24 [21,25]; 86:2; II Sam. 22:21-25). There is no contradiction. Although the *yetzer ha-ra*, the "evil inclination" is operative, we *can* be righteous. Human sinfulness is not connected to Adam. Repentance, not "vicarious atonement," erases sin-guilt: "For you have no delight in sacrifice. The sacrifice acceptable to God is a broken spirit…" (vv. 16,17).

Ps. 58:3: "The wicked go astray from the womb; they err from their birth, speaking lies." Not a universal indictment. The Psalmist is speaking of the "wicked" and "liars."

Ps. 82:6,7: "I have said, 'You are gods; and all of you are children of the most High.' But you shall die like man [*k'adam*]…" Cf. "They like man [*k'adam*] violated the covenant; there they acted treacherously against me" (Hos. 6:7): *K'adam*='like mortals.' This is not a reference to the first Adam but to mankind (cf. Ps. 116:11; Prov. 20:6).

Ps. 130:3,4: "If you, YHVH, would take account of sins, Lord, who could stand? But there is forgiveness with you." "Enter not into judgment with your servant; for no man living is righteous before you" (Ps 143:2). But only three Psalms later we read of God's love for the righteous (Ps. 146:8)!—Because sinfulness is human, God is forgiving. God said to Noah: "You have I seen righteous before me *in this generation*" (Gen. 7:1 cf. 6:9). Noah's righteousness was judged *against his generation*. Man can never measure up to God's perfect standard. Considering his human limitations, however, and measuring him against other humans, he may be "righteous." His righteousness, therefore, is *qualified* or *conditional*, not *absolute*.

Prov. 20:9: "Who can say, 'I have made my heart clean; I am pure from my sin?'" The obvious answer is, no one. But man *can* be righteous; righteousness does not presuppose perfection: "A righteous man who walks in his integrity— blessed are his sons after him" (Prov. 20:7). Righteousness is dynamic. The righteous go "from strength to strength" (Ps. 84:7), ever learning and accumulating merit through righteous deeds: "The path of the righteous is as a shining light which grows steadily brighter until full day" (Prov. 4:18).

Eccl. 7:20: "There is not a righteous person on earth who does good and sins not." This does not preclude the existence of righteous persons. Indeed, there *are* righteous persons, but they are not perfect.

Eccl. 7:29: "God has made man upright, but *they* [not Adam, but the race] have sought out many devices." The transgression in Eden is not blamed! Mankind is not created *perfect*, but upright—with the potential to be righteous or evil.

Isa. 43:27: "Your first father sinned, and your mediators transgressed against me." The reference is to Jacob-Israel (I Chron. 29:10). Verse 28 confirms that the "father" is Jacob and the mediators are the Levite priests.

Jer. 17:9,10: "The heart is deceitful above all things, and desperately corrupt; who can understand it?…I YHVH search the mind and try the heart, to give to every man according to his way, according to the fruit of his doings." Adam is not blamed; the deceitful heart is in man's nature. Judgment is based on individual merit. The good inclination can overcome the evil and God rewards accordingly. Notwithstanding the prophet's harsh indictment, he prays: "Heal me, O YHVH, and I shall be healed; save me, and I shall be saved" (v.14).

Lam. 5:7,21: "Our fathers sinned, and are no more; and we bear their iniquities…Restore us to yourself, O YHVH, that we may be restored! Renew our days as of old." Again, Adam is not blamed. Although we may suffer the consequences of the sins of ancestors, restoration is possible.

Job 4:17,18: 15:14,15; 25:4,5: "Can mortal man be righteous before God? Can a man be pure before his Maker?" These are the words of Eliphaz and Bildad, Job's pseudo-comforters, against whom Job inveighs: "You whitewash with lies; worthless physicians are you all…Will you speak falsely for God…Your maxims are proverbs of ashes…Miserable comforters are you all" (13:4,7,12; 16:2; 21:34). Finally, God accuses Job's faithless friends: "You have not spoken of me what is right, as my servant Job has" (42:7) Indeed, the speeches of Job's false comforters are a mixture of truths and distortions, presenting a cynical and unbalanced picture of the universe. Yes, man who is of the dust is imperfect, prone to sin and mortal. But it is a cynical exaggeration to say man cannot be righteous before God, that he is but a "maggot and a worm" (25:6)—although that is his ultimate destination. Scripture is optimistic about man's potential: God tells Israel, "Be holy for I am holy" (Lev. 12:44,45).

The Psalmist says: "Who shall ascend the hill of YHVH? And who shall stand in his holy place? He who has clean hands and a pure heart, who does not lift up his soul to what is false, and does not swear deceitfully" (Ps. 24:3,4). Noah is "a righteous man, blameless in his generation" (Gen. 6:9; 7:1). David says, "YHVH rewarded me according to my righteousness; according to the cleanness of my hands he recompensed me…I was blameless before him, and I kept myself from guilt" (Ps. 18:20-24; cf. 97:11). These latter statements are in stark contrast with the cynicism of Job's detractors! But even in their cynicism, Job's "friends" do not connect human sinfulness and mortality with Adam. Man is by nature imperfect; human sinfulness is not extraordinary—even the heavenly hosts are imperfect. We are not condemned for our imperfect state any more than the heavenly hosts. Because there is no condemnation, there is no need for a scheme of "Christian salvation"—only compassion from a God who understands our nature (Ps. 103:13,14). God alone is perfect. Sinfulness is the natural state of mortal man made from the dust, not the consequence of Adam's sin. Surely, the "Original Sin" advocates would not argue that the angelic hosts were infected by the sin of some primeval being.

Nonetheless, we are cautioned against "*self*-righteousness": "Most men will boast of their own goodness, but a faithful man, who can find" (Prov. 20:7). God detests presumptuousness, arrogance and *super*—piety (Prov. 8:13; Eccl. 7:16). The mark of a truly righteous man is humility (Mic. 6:8).

Job 14:1–6: "Man born of woman is of few days, and full of trouble...do you open your eyes upon such a one and bring him into judgment with you? Who can bring a clean thing out of an unclean? There is not one. Since his days are determined look away from him, and desist, that he may enjoy, like a hireling, his day" (vv. 1—6). Job's plaint *seems* like that of his false comforters, as he shares with them the notion of the fragileness and temporality of human life. But there are significant differences: Job adds the dimension of divine compassion and forgiveness. We are by nature mortal. Our mortality is not due to ancestral sin; we are not condemnable for that which is natural to us. Job, therefore, seeks divine leniency.

(Note—"Man born of a *woman*, not "Adam." The expression has no theological overtones. It means simply, humanity, and is similar to the expression, "son of man" Compare our discussion above on Hosea 6:7.) [Scholars question the validity of v. 4, believing it to be a marginal gloss (Anchor Bible).]

Despite the bleak assessment of man in Job, we must not forget God's own appraisal of Job: "There is none like him on the earth, a blameless and upright man, who fears God and turns away from evil" (1:8; 2:3). At the end, Job is rewarded (42:10). In Ezek. 14:20, Job, though Adam's descendant, is linked with righteous Noah and Daniel.

In none of the above references to man's sinful nature or mortality is there any mention of the Eden Story. The Psalmist knows nothing of "original sin." There is universal sinfulness but not *hereditary guilt*. The evil inclination was *created* in Adam, not caused by his sin. Otherwise, he could not have been tempted.

HUMAN POTENTIAL FOR RIGHTEOUSNESS

Hebrew Scripture does not share the Christian Scriptures' cynical view of man as depraved and incapable of righteousness: Psalms: "He saves the upright in heart" (7:11). "He loves righteousness; the upright shall behold his face" (11:7). "The eyes of YHVH are toward the righteous" (24:15 [16]). "Integrity and uprightness shall preserve me" (25:21). "YHVH upholds the righteous" (37:17). "I have not seen a righteous person abandoned" (37:25). "Mark the perfect man and behold the upright for the end of that man is peace" (37:37). "The salvation of the righteous is from YHVH" (37:39). "There is a reward for the righteous" (58:11 [12]). "The righteous shall flourish like the palm tree" (92:12 [13]). "The righteous shall be for an eternal remembrance" (112:6). "The upright shall dwell in your presence" (140:14). "The LORD loves righteous persons" (146:8). "Blessings are upon the head of the righteous" (Prov. 10:6). "The memory of the righteous is for a blessing" (Prov. 10:7). "The activity of the righteous is for life" (Prov. 10:16). "The righteous shall never be moved" (Prov. 10:30; 12:3). "The righteousness of the perfect shall direct his way. The righteousness of the upright delivers them" (Prov. 11:5,6). "The fruit of the righteous is a tree of life. Behold, the righteous shall be repaid in the earth" (Prov. 11:30,31). "The house of the righteous shall stand" (Prov. 12:7). "His pleasure is in the prayer of the righteous" (Prov. 15:8). "The righteous goes about in his integrity" (Prov. 20:7). "A righteous man may fall seven times and arise" (Prov. 24:16). "Light is sown for the righteous" (Prov. 58:12). "The righteous lives in his integrity" (Hab. 20:7).

RIGHTEOUS INDIVIDUALS BEFORE JESUS

Despite Paul's teaching that "all men…are under the power of sin" (Rom. 3:9,10), Scripture mentions a number of righteous individuals: *Abel* (Mt. 23:35; I Jn. 3:12); *Enoch* (Gen. 5:22); *Noah* (Gen. 6:9; 7:1); *Abraham* (Gen. 15:6; 17:1; II Chron. 20:7; Isa. 41:8). *Moses* (Num. 12:7,8; Deut. 34:10); *Job* (Job 1:1,8); *David* (I Sam. 22:21–25; Ps. 18:20–24; 86:2); *Jeremiah* (1:5); and *Daniel* (Ezek. 14:14,20). And what of Moses and Elijah? They appear in the "transfiguration" (Matt. 17:3)! And this was *prior* to the "atonement" of Jesus!

GUILT AND MERIT BY ASSOCIATION

Scripture knows of *limited* guilt by association, as well as *merit* by association: Ham's descendants are cursed because of Ham's disrespect toward Noah, whereas Shem and Japheth's descendants are blessed (Gen. 9:22–27). God punishes the children for the fathers' sins "to the third and the fourth generation of those who hate me" (Exod. 20:5). But God is also merciful and gracious, slow to anger, and abounding in steadfast love and faithfulness, keeping steadfast love for thousands, forgiving iniquity and transgression and sin…and his righteousness is to children's children, to those who keep his covenant and remember to do his commandments" (Exod. 34:6,7; Num. 14:18,19; Deut. 5:9; Ps. 103:17,18): Only the guilt of those who *hate* God is transmitted—and only to the fourth generation! Sin is freely forgiven, without any so-called "vicarious atonement" (Hos. 14:4). The "guilty" are punished; but "thousands" receive God's love and forgiveness.

The merit of the ancestors redounds to their descendants: "By your descendants all the nations of the earth shall bless themselves" (Gen. 26:2–5). "And God remembered his covenant with Abraham, with Isaac, and with Jacob. And God saw the people of Israel, and God knew their condition" (Exod. 2:24,25; cf. Ps. 106:42,43,45; Exod. 32:13; Lev. 26:42). "I have set before you life and death, blessing and curse; therefore choose life, that you and *your descendants* may live" (Deut. 30:19). "A righteous man who walks in his integrity—blessed *are his sons after* him" (Prov. 20:7).

INDIVIDUAL RESPONSIBILITY, NOT COLLECTIVE GUILT

We are not condemned because of ancestral guilt but are judged on individual merit: "Whoever has sinned against me, him will I blot out of my book" (Exod. 32:33; cf. Nu. 16:22). "The fathers shall not be put to death for the children, nor shall the children be put to death for the fathers; every man shall be put to death for his own sin" (Deut. 24:16; II Ki. 14:6; Jer. 31:29,30; Ezek. 18:19,20; 33:19,20). "[He rewards] every man according to his ways and according to the fruit of his doings" (Jer. 17:10; 32:19). "Judge me, O YHVH, according to my righteousness and according to the integrity that is in me" (Ps. 7:8). "*Your* iniquities have made a separation between you and your God" (Isa. 59:2). It is not "Adamic sin" that separates us from God but our *own* iniquities. Those who keep God's law are blessed with abundant life: "I gave them my statutes and showed them my ordinances, by whose observance man shall live" (Ezek. 20:11-13,18).

THE TALMUD ON "ORIGINAL SIN"

"Your entry into the world is without sin" (Baba Metsia 107a). "Know you that the Holy One is pure, his angels are pure and the soul which He gave you is pure" (Niddah 30 b). "As God is pure, so the soul is pure" (Berachot 11). "God made man upright but they [not Adam] have sought out many inventions" (Eccl. 7:29; Leviticus Rabah 14:5). "Your deeds will bring you near [to God] and your deeds will remove you" (Eduyot 5:47).

SUMMARY

EDEN STORY DOES NOT SUPPORT HEREDITARY GUILT

The Christian doctrine of "Original Sin," (Rom. 5:12; I Cor. 15:22), is based on a misunderstanding of the Eden story and is unsupported by Scripture. God's warning to Adam, "In the day you eat of [the forbidden fruit] you shall surely die" (Gen. 2:17), did not mean the loss of immortality; Adam was *created* mortal! *Adam* means "earthling"; that which is of the earth returns to the earth (Gen. 3:19; I Cor. 15:53). The penalty for disobedience was premature death, but the penalty was mercifully rescinded (Gen. 8:21; 18:23-33; Exod. 32:12–14). The Eden story says nothing about the transmission of "sin-guilt" to Adam's descendants. Scripture is opposed to "collective or hereditary guilt" (Gen. 18:23, 25; Ezek. 18:17; Exod. 32:33). Despite Adam's disobedience, he had righteous descendants: Enoch, Noah, Abraham, Job, etc. (Prov. 20:7). Man is not condemned to depravity.

FREE TO CHOOSE GOOD OR EVIL

God tells Cain that sin can be conquered (Gen. 4:7). Although Scripture often refers to human sinfulness, the Garden of Eden story is never again referred to. To say man is a sinner is an inaccurate and incomplete description of man. There is a "sinful inclination" and a "good inclination" and we must constantly strive to overcome the "sinful inclination" (Ps. 19:13). We are free to choose between good and evil (Deut. 30:19). What is expected of us is not sinlessness but sincere striving after righteousness (Mic. 6:8). Man is judged by deeds (Nu. 14:19,20; Ps. 24:3–5; 51:10; Jer. 17:10; cf. Acts 10:35).

FORGIVENESS OF SIN AVAILABLE BEFORE JESUS

Salvation and forgiveness of sin were available before Jesus, without sacrifice (Gen. 49:18; Exod. 14:13; Deut. 4:7; 7:14; 33:29; I Ki. 8:30; Ps. 25:18; Mic. 7:18). In Christianity "sin" is a condition; in Judaism it is an act. Christianity emphasizes man's sinfulness and depravity; Judaism emphasizes his potential. By emphasizing God's merciful recognition of man's limitation, Judaism honors God and encourages human striving. God's handiwork is not a failure in need of divine rescue. A loving God would not punish billions for one ancestor's misdeed (cf. Jn. 3:16).

"ORIGINAL-SIN" DISHONORS GOD

The doctrine of "original sin" portrays God as unjust, punishing the innocent for the guilty (Deut. 32:4). God's righteous law, not "vicarious atonement," is the remedy for human sinfulness: "For the ways of YHVH are right and the righteous shall walk in them" (Hos. 14:9). "Let your heart keep my commandments, for length of days and long life and peace shall they add to you" (Prov. 3:2).

CHAPTER 11

THE "RANSOM SACRIFICE"

In the chapter on "Original Sin," we pointed out that in Christian theology the remedy for sin and death is the "Ransom Sacrifice," the death of a perfect human to compensate for "Adam's sin." (Mt. 20:28; Mk. 10:45; Jn. 3:16; Mt. 26:26-28; 1 Tim. 2:6). In the present chapter, we shall demonstrate that the "Ransom Sacrifice" is pagan.

"BINDING OF ISAAC" NOT A TYPE OF CRUCIFIXION

In Christian theology, the "binding of Isaac," the *akedah,* typifies the crucifixion (Jn. 1:29; Jn. 3:16; Acts 8:32). This event, however, teaches the very opposite, namely, that God does *not* want human sacrifice. Moreover, the *akedah* was not about atonement but was a test of Abraham's worthiness to father a great nation.

The old version renders Gen. 22:8,13: "And Abraham said, God will provide himself a lamb for a burnt offering." The missionary interpretation of this is: "God *himself* will be the sacrifice." This interpretation, with its implications of Incarnation and Trinity, is erroneous and misrepresents the original Hebrew: The correct translation is: "God himself will see to the lamb for the offering." Also, how does Jesus fit the metaphor of a "burnt offering" (Mk. 16:6; Acts 1:3,9; 2:31,32)? Another incongruity: Abraham offers up a *ram*! This verse is never quoted by missionaries because the not so docile "ram" is not a useful type of Jesus.

HUMAN SACRIFICE ABHORRENT TO GOD

Human sacrifice is abhorrent to God. God's rejection of Abraham's intended sacrifice of Isaac was an object-lesson, demonstrating God's repugnance of human sacrifice (Gen. 22). "You shall not give any of your children to devote them by fire to Molech" (Lev. 18:21; 20:2–5). "You shall not do so to YHVH your God; forevery abominable thing which YHVH hates they have done for their gods; for they even burn their sons and daughters in the fire to their gods" (Deut. 12:31; 18:10; 2 Ki. 3:26,27). "They have filled this place with the blood of innocents, and have built the high places of Baal to burn their sons in the fire as burnt offerings for Baal, which I did not command or decree, nor did it come into my mind" (Jer. 19:4,5; Ps. 106:37,38). The first-born sons of Israel were redeemed by substitute animal-sacrifices as a protest against human sacrifice (Exod. 13:15).

JESUS' "SACRIFICE" NOT VALID

Jesus' "sacrifice" was not a true sacrifice. Jesus knew he would receive his life back in three days and be restored to his former glory: "I lay down my life, that I may take it again". (Jn. 10:17,18; Mt. 16:21; Lu. 9:22; Jn. 2:19–21; Php. 2:9; Mt. 24:30; 25:31; Heb. 2:9; Rev. 5:12). Since nothing was lost, Jesus' death was not a sacrifice: "And this is the will of him who sent me, that I should lose nothing of all that he has given me, but raise it up at the last day" (Jn. 6:39).

Jesus' alleged sacrifice, having not been consumed by fire, was ritually unacceptable: "You shall let none of it remain until the morning. Anything that remains until the morning you shall burn" (Exod. 12:10; I Cor. 5:7; cf. Gen. 22:2,13; Exod. 29:18; Lev. 1:9; I Ki. 18:38).

It is not clear who offered the sacrifice: God (Jn. 3:16; Rom. 8:32); or Jesus (Jn. 6:51; 10:15–18; I Jn. 3:16). The ancient formula for sin-offerings involved three elements: the sacrificer, the object sacrificed and the recipient. The "Ransom Sacrifice" of Jesus does not fit the formula: God sacrifices his own son—to himself—and the sacrifice is taken back—an absurdity!

For Christians, "Without the shedding of blood, there is no remission of sins" (Heb. 9:22; Ron. 5:9; I Jn. 1:7; Rev. 1:5). But in ancient Israel *animal* blood made atonement (Lev. 17:11)! (Only John mentions that Jesus bled [19:31–37].) Moreover, Jesus offered forgiveness of sins *before* his "blood-atonement" (Mt. 9:2; Mk. 2:5; Luke 5:20; 7:48; cf. Mk. 1:4).

ISRAELITE SACRIFICE, A TEMPORARY INSTITUTION

The sacrificial system was temporary, intended to wean Israel from pagan human sacrifice. God's plan for man is not static. For example, at first man was vegetarian; then meat was permitted (Gen. 1:29; 9:4). Animal sacrifice was replaced by prayer, repentance, and good works: "Let my prayer be counted as incense before you and the lifting up of my hands as an evening sacrifice" (Ps. 141:2; cf. Hos. 14:2; Jonah 2:9).

"SACRIFICE AND OFFERING YOU DID NOT DESIRE"

The prophets hoped to move Israel away from sacrifice: "By loyalty and faithfulness iniquity is atoned for" (Prov. 16:6). "Deliver me from bloodguiltiness; O God, the God of my salvation,...For you have no delight in sacrifice; were I to give a burnt offering, you would not be pleased. The sacrifice acceptable to God is a broken spirit; a broken and contrite heart, O God, you will not despise" (Ps. 51:14–17). "Sacrifice and offering you do not desire; but you have given me an open ear. Burnt offering and sin offering you have not required" (Ps. 40:6). "Do I eat the flesh of bulls or drink the blood of goats? Offer to God a sacrifice of thanksgiving [prayer]" (Ps. 50:13,14,23). "I will praise the name of God with singing and I will magnify him with thanksgiving. And it shall please YHVH more than an ox that has horns and hoofs" (Ps. 69:30,31). "To do righteousness and justice is more acceptable to YHVH than sacrifice" (Prov. 21:3). "And Samuel said, 'Has YHVH as great delight in burnt offerings and sacrifices, as in obeying the voice of YHVH? Behold, to obey is better than sacrifice, and to hearken than the fat of rams'" (I Sam. 15:22).

"I DESIRE MERCY AND NOT SACRIFICE"

"For I desire mercy and not sacrifice, the knowledge of God more than burnt offerings" (Hos. 6:6). "With what shall I come before YHVH, and bow myself before God on high? Shall I come before him with burnt offerings, with calves a year old? Will YHVH be pleased with thousands of rams, with ten thousands of rivers of oil? Shall I give my first-born for my transgression, the fruit of my body for the sin of my soul? He has showed you, O man, what is good and what YHVH requires of you but to do justice, and to love kindness, and to walk humbly with your God" (Mic. 6:6–8).

"THOUGH YOUR SINS BE AS SCARLET, THEY SHALL BE WHITE AS SNOW"

To forsake evil and pursue righteousness is more acceptable to God than sacrifice: "What to me is the multitude of your sacrifices? says YHVH; I have had enough of burnt offerings of rams and the fat of fed beasts; I do not delight in the blood of bulls, or of lambs, or of hegoats...Wash yourselves; make yourselves clean; remove the evil of your doings from before my eyes; cease to do evil, learn to do good; seek justice, correct oppression; defend the fatherless, plead for the widow. Come now, let us reason together, says YHVH: though your sins be as scarlet, they shall be as white as snow; though they be red like crimson, they shall be as wool" (Isa. 1:11–18). "Let the wicked forsake his way, and the unrighteous man his thoughts; let him return to YHVH, that he may have mercy upon him, and to our God, for he will abundantly pardon" (Isa. 55:7). "If a man is righteous and does what is lawful and right...he shall surely live, says YHVH" (Ezek. 18:5–9). Moses offered his life on behalf of Israel but God refused it. God holds each one responsible for his own deeds (Exod. 32:30–33; cf. also Ps 69:30,31; 107:22; 116:17; 141:2; Hos. 14:2; Jonah 2:9).

CHRISTIAN "COMMUNION" AND THE MOSAIC BLOOD-PROHIBITION

Jesus compared the wine of the Passover meal to his blood (Mt. 26:26-28; Mk. 14:23,24; Jn. 6:53-55). Even as symbolism, this violates the spirit of Scripture. The eating of blood was strictly prohibited (Gen. 9:4; Lev. 17:10; 3:17; 7–26,27; 19:26; Deut. 12:16,23-25). The blood of the sacrifice was to be poured out to prevent the sacrificer from partaking of it (Lev. 8:15; Deut. 12:27).

"RANSOM SACRIFICE" PAGAN; REPUGNANT TO GOD

Some characterize the "Hebrew God" as vengeful and the "Christian God" as loving. But what is more unloving than a human sacrifice and more vengeful than penalizing children for an ancestor's sin! This is a cruel and preposterous notion, borrowed from paganism.

"RANSOM SACRIFICE" UNNECESSARY

The first man was not created perfect, otherwise he could not have sinned. God does not demand sinlessness from imperfect man; He demands only righteousness. With no condemnation for innate sinfulness, there is no need for a "Ransom Sacrifice." Repentance and good deeds atone (Jer. 17:10).

"LOVINGKINDNESS NOT SACRIFICE"

There are those who reject the doctrine of eternal torment in everlasting hell-fire claiming it characterizes God as a merciless fiend. The "Ransom Sacrifice" is equally fiendish. The prophet has a more just and humane solution: "For I desire lovingkindness and not sacrifice; and the knowledge of God more than burnt offerings" (Hos. 6:6). God does not exact an impossible price from imperfect man—only sincere repentance and a return to right conduct: "I will love [you] *freely.*"

CHAPTER 12

MEDIATOR

In Christianity, the "sinner's" access to God is through Jesus: "There is one mediator between God and men, the man Christ Jesus" (I Tim. 2:5; Jn. 14:6).

INTERCESSIONS OF THE PATRIARCHS

Intercessory prayer is not alien to Israelite religion. Abraham petitioned God on behalf of the righteous in the condemned cities of Sodom and Gomorrah (Gen. 18:23–33; cf. 20:7). Moses interceded for Israel (Exod. 32:30–32; Ps. 106:23; cf. Amos 7:1—6). Job prayed for his friends (Job 42:7–9). When the Israelites asked Samuel to pray for them, he consented, but admonished: "Only fear YHVH, and serve him faithfully with all your heart..." (I Sam. 12:19-25). He directed the people toward God, away from himself. Samuel's response underscores the significant difference between the intercessions of the Patriarchs and that of Jesus. The Patriarchs never arrogated divine prerogatives to themselves. Whereas the Christian messiah forgives sin, in Hebrew Scripture, God *alone* forgives sin:

"I acknowledged my sin to you...then you forgave the guilt of my sin" (Ps. 32:5; 103:3; Isa. 43:25; Dan. 9:9). The Christian's access to God is only through Jesus; the Israelite *personally* entreated God's forgiveness—without a *mediator*!

"FOR GOD ALONE MY SOUL WAITS"

Israel did not need a mediator; God was present with his people: "And they shall make me a sanctuary and I will dwell among them" (Exod. 25:8). "What great nation is there that has a god so near to it as YHVH our God is to us, whenever we call upon him!" (Deut. 4:7). "For God alone my soul waits in silence; from him comes my salvation"...(Ps. 62:1,5). "YHVH is near to all who call upon him, to all who call upon him in truth" (Ps. 145:18). "All who call upon the name of YHVH shall be delivered" (Joel 2:32). "For thus says the high and lofty One whose name is Holy; I dwell in the high and holy place, and also with him who is of a contrite and humble spirit, to revive the spirit of the humble, and to revive the heart of the contrite" (Isa. 57:15).

"FEAR YHVH AND SWEAR BY *HIS* NAME"

For Christians, the only name under heaven by which one may be saved is Jesus (Acts 4:12). Whereas the Jew declares: "YHVH, other lords besides you have ruled over us, *but your name alone we acknowledge*" (Isa. 26:13), "Messianic Jews" pray, "*B'shem Yeshua Ha-Mashiach*" ("In the name of Jesus the Messiah"). But the Jew "blesses himself by the God of truth" (Isa. 65:16). Those who pray in the name of the "god-man" should heed the admonition: "Make no mention of the names of other gods, nor let such be heard out of your mouth" (Exod. 23:13). "You shall fear YHVH your God and serve him and you shall swear by *his* name" (Deut. 6:13; Jer. 3:23; 12:16; Zech. 10:12).

CHRISTIANITY "REGRESSED"

Israel progressed from image-worship to one, invisible God. Christianity *regressed* when an intercessor became necessary to approach God.

CHAPTER 13

LAW COVENANT

"I HAVE NOT COME TO DESTROY BUT TO FULFILL"

Jesus said: "Do not think I have come to destroy the law or the prophets; I have not come to destroy but to fulfill. For truly I say to you, till heaven and earth pass away, not an iota, not a dot, will pass from the law until all is fulfilled. Whoever, therefore, shall break one of these least commandments, and shall teach men so, he shall be called least in the kingdom of heaven. But whoever shall do and teach them, that one shall be called great in the kingdom of heaven" (Mt. 5:17–19).

Is Jesus enjoining the Mosaic Law upon Christians? One commentary states: "These verses have caused considerable difficulty because they seem to demand a total acceptance of the OT law in a way which was neither practiced by the early church nor apparently advocated in the rest of the Sermon on the Mount... *To fulfill* is probably not so much to obey them as to 'give them their full meaning'...Law and prophets find their deepest significance when the Messiah comes (*New Bible Commentary*, third edition, Guthrie, Motyer, 1970) . Another commentary states: "Jesus was never accused of destroying the moral teaching of the prophets...His mission is to preserve it by revealing its depth of meaning, by carrying it forward into that which it had been designed to bring about—the Kingdom of God" (*Peak's Commentary on the Bible*, 1919).

The above commentaries reflect the dilemma of reconciling Jesus' apparent affirmation of the Mosaic Law with Paul's abolition of it. The commentators are saying several things: (1) Jesus' mission was not to teach compliance with the

Mosaic Law but to interpret its deeper meaning or essence—love of God and neighbor (Mt. 22:36-40). (2) Jesus came to teach the "moral" Law but abolished the "ceremonial" Law. (3) The Law was intended to bring Israel to Messiah-Christ, the object or fulfillment of the Law (Gal. 3:24,25).

The above represents the classic position of the Church regarding the Mosaic Law. Where do "Hebrew Christians" stand?

"HEBREW CHRISTIAN" POSITION ON LAW AMBIGUOUS

Arnold Fruchtenbaum, a "Hebrew Christian," states: "The Law of Moses has been rendered inoperative with the death of Christ (Rom. 10:4; Gal. 2:16; Heb. 7:19). "The Law of Moses, especially as represented by the Ten Commandments, is a ministration of death and...condemnation...We are under a new law...the Law of Christ...totally separate from the Law of Moses."

While categorically rejecting the Mosaic Law, in keeping with Pauline Christianity, Fruchtenbaum concedes that Festival-observance can be useful: "They are good opportunities to share the faith with unbelieving Jewish people, showing how the particular feast points to the Messiahship of Christ" (*Hebrew Christianity*, pp. 83, 107).

David Chernoff, a "Messianic Jew," is more accepting of the Mosaic Law, although ambiguous: "Do Messianic Jews believe they should keep the Law of Moses? Yes and no. The Torah (or Law of Moses) is composed of the 613 Mitzvot, or commandments that God gave to Moses on Mount Sinai...Gentile Christianity today maintains that the Law is completely dead. We, as Messianic Jews, recognize that one cannot be saved through the Law...At the same time, while the Law cannot save, it is far from being dead. The moral precepts are carried into the New Covenant. The Festivals are for eternity, [the Sabbath]...was instituted before the Law was given, as was tithing...[Paul] makes it very clear that all believers have liberty in the Messiah Yeshua (Gal. 5:1), which means freedom from the Law as well as freedom to keep the Law...[Paul] kept the Law as much as he could...When we, as Messianic Jews, celebrate the festivals, we do so in a Messianic way, with the view that Yeshua is the fulfillment of all of these Holy Days (i.e., He is our Passover Lamb, our Atonement on Yom Kippur, etc.)...Most Messianic Jews celebrate the Biblical festivals...because it is instructed by God in the Torah for Israel to observe these festivals forever, (Lev. 23:21,31,41; Exod. 12:14)" (*Messianic Judaism*, pp. 17, 18, 14,).

Chernoff is somewhere between Fruchtenbaum and Pauline Christianity. For Fruchtenbaum the Law is dead. For Chernoff, although the Law cannot save, its "moral" precepts are operative: Tithing, Sabbath, Festivals and Yom Kippur are "useful," so long as they embody meaning relating to "Yeshua-Messiah." But

Chernoff's equation leaves out the Torah's dietary regulations, which are included in the "forever" formula! (Deut. 12:28; 29:29)

In the Gospel of Luke, we are told that Zechariah and Elizabeth, the parents of John the Baptist, "were both righteous before God, walking in all the commandments and ordinances of the Lord, blameless" (Luke 1:6). David Stern, a "Messianic Jew" living in Israel, commenting on this verse, says: "Contrary to some Christian theologians, the New Testament teaches that the Torah of Moses offers righteousness" (p. 103, *Jewish New Testament Commentary*, 1992). Despite this startling departure from traditional Pauline Christianity, Stern makes no comment on Rom. 4:13: "The promise to Abraham and his descendants did not come through the law but through the righteousness of faith." Nor does Stern comment on Col. 2:14: "Having canceled the bond which stood against us with its legal demands; this he set aside, nailing it to the cross". Stern adroitly sidesteps this anti-Torah statement!

What is Stern's position on the Mosaic dietary laws? Commenting on Rom. 14:14, "I know and am persuaded in the Lord Jesus that nothing is unclean in itself," Stern states: "Developing a messianic Jewish theology of ritual impurity is beyond the scope of this commentary" (p. 436). Stern's ambivalence is also evident in the following: "Until Messianic Judaism has a clearer idea of what being Jewish in a Messianic setting means, it seems premature to convert Gentiles, enjoining them to observe the entire Torah before we ourselves have reached some consensus about what the 'entire Torah,' understood from a New Testament viewpoint, is" (p. 563). Elsewhere Stern says: "The Torah today is the Torah of the Messiah…it includes the Messiah's mitzvot…The NT names a new group with authority to interpret it" (p. 146). For Stern the Torah is no longer the Torah of Moses and the Jews!

Commenting on James 1:25, "the perfect law, the law of liberty," Stern writes: "But is the *Torah* of Moses, then, incomplete, less than perfect? Of course not. It was God's perfect, complete and sufficient revelation to mankind at the point in history when it was given. Later, 'when the appointed time arrived, God sent forth his Son' (Gal. 4:4) to initiate the New Covenant and provide further revelation and instruction (Torah), adding to and completing…the *Torah* which was already perfect" (pp. 727, 728). For Jews, the Torah *still* is "God's perfect, complete and sufficient revelation."

PRO-LAW POSITION OF "MESSIANIC JUDAISM" CRITICIZED

The pro-Law position of "Messianic Judaism" has received criticism from certain "Hebrew Christian" quarters: "There are many 20-century Judaizers who foster a works-righteousness religious system among undiscerning believers…believing their salvation and sanctification are not complete unless they follow certain legalistic requirements. Christians must be vigilant and guard against deceivers..." (*Israel My Glory*, Oct./Nov., 1992; Feb./Mar. 1993).

IS JESUS ADVOCATING TORAH-OBSERVANCE IN MT. 5:17-20?

Returning to Mt. 5:17-20: "Do not think I have come to destroy the law or the prophets; I have not come to destroy but to fulfill (17). For truly I say to you, till heaven and earth pass away, not an iota, not a dot, will pass from the law until all is fulfilled (18). Whoever, therefore, breaks one of these least commandments, and teaches men so, he shall be called least in the kingdom of heaven (19). Unless your righteousness exceeds that of the scribes and Pharisees, you will never enter the kingdom of heaven" (20). Verse 17, taken by itself, could mean: "I, Jesus, am the fulfillment of the Law and prophets, that is, of their "messianic prophecies." (Cf. Luke 24:44.) But vv. 18, 19 would alter this interpretation, for they speak of observance and non-observance of the commandments. *Now* Jesus seems to be advocating commandment-keeping, the expression "till heaven and earth pass away" signifying "endlessly" (cf. Gen. 8:22). However, the commandments that Jesus goes on to discuss are the "moral" commandments: Murder, Adultery, False Oaths, Eye for Eye, Love of Neighbor, Giving Alms, Prayer, Fasting. With the possible exception of Fasting, no ritual laws are mentioned, viz., Sabbath, festivals, dietary regulations, etc. When Jesus ends his sermon, "the crowds [are) astonished at his teaching for he taught them as one having authority and not as the scribes"—insinuating that *Jesus'* authority superceded that of the Jewish teachers of the Law. Further undermining the authority of the Rabbis, Jesus says (v. 20): "Unless your righteousness exceeds that of the scribes and Pharisees, you will never enter the kingdom of heaven." Thereupon, Jesus gives a new and more stringent interpretation of the Mosaic Law, concluding: "You therefore, must be perfect, as your heavenly Father is perfect." Jesus has not "abolished" the Law of Moses but *reinterpreted* it!

If, therefore, Jesus upheld the Law, why did he denounce its teachers: "Beware...of the teaching of the Pharisees and Sadducees" (Mt. 16:11,12)? Jesus said the Law ended with John the Baptist (Mt. 11:13) and in Mt. 15:11, Jesus seems to set aside the dietary laws (cf. Rom. 14:20). John says: "The law was given through Moses; grace and truth came through Jesus Christ" (1:17). Peter dispenses with the Mosaic dietary laws and calls circumcision an unbearable "yoke" (Acts 10:9-15; ch. 15).

But the conjectures about Jesus' attitude regarding the Law grow academic before the unequivocal anti-Law position of Paul, whom the Church and the majority of Christians follow. Jesus said the Law would not pass until "all is ful-filled." According to Paul, when is all "fulfilled"?

PAUL AND THE LAW

Paul answers: Jesus' death ended the law: "You have died to the law through the body of Christ" (Rom. 7:4,6; Rom. 10:4; Eph. 2:15; Col. 2:14). Paul was anti-Law: "You are not under the Law but under grace" (Rom. 6:14; cf. I Cor. 9:20; Gal. 5:18; Php. 3:9). "The law of the spirit of life in Christ Jesus has set me free from the law of sin and death. For God has done what the law, weakened by the flesh, could not do" (Rom. 8:2,3). "The written code kills, but the spirit gives life" (II Cor. 3:6). "By works of the law shall no one be justified...I through the law died to the law...If justification were through the law, Christ died in vain...All who rely on works of the law are under a curse...Christ redeemed us from the curse of the law" (Gal. 2:16,19; 3:10,11,13; cf. Rom. 3:20,28; 4:13–16; Heb. 7:19; Acts 13:39). "[The law] was added because of transgressions, till the offspring should come to whom the promise had been made. The law was our schoolmaster to bring us to Christ, that we might be justified by faith. But after faith is come, we are no longer under a schoolmaster" (Gal. 3:19,24,25). "Let no one pass judgment on you in questions of food and drink or with regard to a fes-tival or a new moon or a Sabbath. These are only a shadow of what is to come; but the substance is of Christ" (Col. 2:16,17; Heb. 8:5–7; 10:1). Paul discour-aged "slavish" observance of holy days and circumcision (Gal. 4:9,10; 5:1,6; 6:15). The dietary laws are dispensed with (Rom. 14:14,17,20; I Cor. l0:25–27; Col. 2:16–23; I Tim. 4:4; Tit. 1:14,15; Heb. 9:9,10).

In the following, Paul appears to be a Law-observing Jew: "I worship the God of our fathers, believing everything laid down by the law or written in the prophets" (Acts 24:14). Does this make Paul a Mosaic-Law keeper? Paul says "believing," not "doing"! Is Paul talking about Law-observance or messianic prophecy" (cf. Mt. 11:13; Lu. 16:16; 24:44)? Paul says, "Neither against the law of the Jews have I offended at all" (Acts 25:8)—A grudging statement—"law of the Jews"! Why not "law of Moses"? In Gal. 1:13, Paul refers to his "former life in Judaism": "I advanced in Judaism beyond many of my own age among my peo-ple, so extremely zealous was I for the traditions of my fathers" (Gal. l:13,14)—But he speaks of his "zealous law-keeping" as in *the past!* Paul asks, "Are they Hebrew? So am I. Are they Israelites? So am I. Are they descendants of Abraham? So am I" (II Cor. 11:22). One would wish Paul had said, "Are they Jews? So am I." In v. 24, Paul seems to disassociate himself from the Jews! In I Cor 9:20, Paul clearly states that he is *not* under the law. When we weigh the few passages that suggest Paul kept the Law against a much larger body of anti-Law statements, law-abolition wins out! So whether Jesus upheld the Law or not, the fact remains that the church followed Paul.

"ALL" HAS NOT BEEN FULFILLED!

Jesus said the Law would not pass "till all be fulfilled." Has *all* been fulfilled? Christians still await Jesus' second coming to end sin and establish an everlasting kingdom of righteousness (Dan. 2:44; 9:24; Isa. 9:6,7). The Mosaic Law Covenant, therefore, remains in force. Those who advocate its suspension are, in Jesus own words, "least in the kingdom of heaven ; whereas those who keep the Law are great in the kingdom of heaven."

"GREAT PEACE HAVE THEY WHICH LOVE YOUR LAW"

Paul considered the Law slavery (Rom. 7:6; 8:2,3; 2 Cor. 3:6; Gal. 5:1,6; 6:15). But the Law was lovingly kept by Israel: "And now, Israel, what does YHVH your God require of you, but to fear YHVH your God, to walk in all his ways, to *love him*, to serve YHVH your God with all your heart and with all your soul, and to keep the commandments and statutes of YHVH" (Deut. 10:12,13; 13:3,4). The Law was not an insuperable burden, impossible to keep: "For this commandment which I command you this day is not too hard for you nor is it far off. It is not in the heavens, as if to say, who shall go up for us to heaven and get it for us that we may hear it and do it?...But the word is very near to you, in your mouth and in your heart to do it" (Deut. 30:11-14). For David the Law was a blessing and a delight: "Blessed is the man who walks not in the counsel of the wicked...his delight is in the law of YHVH; on his law he meditates day and night" (Ps. 1:2). Prosperity and success await those who study and follow the Law (Josh. 1:8).

PSALM 119—LOVING ODE TO THE LAW

Psalm 119 is Scripture's most poignant testimony to Israel's love of the Law: "Blessed are those whose way is blameless, who walk in the law of YHVH; who keep his testimonies and seek him with their whole heart. In the way of your testimonies I delight as much as in all riches. Open my eyes, that I may behold wondrous things out of your law. My soul is consumed with longing for your ordinances. Give me understanding, that I may keep your law with my whole heart. I will keep your law continually. I shall walk at liberty, for I have sought your precepts. I revere your commandments, which I love, and I will meditate on your statutes. The law of your mouth is better to me than thousands of gold and silver pieces. I will never forget your precepts; by them you have given me life. Oh how I love your law! It is my meditation all the day. I love your commandments above gold, above fine gold. Great peace have they which love your law; nothing shall offend them." How striking is the contrast between David's exultant hymn and Paul's melancholy characterization of the Law as a curse and yoke of bondage!

Unlike Paul, Daniel did not regard the Law as a curse: "I prayed to YHVH my God and made confession, saying, 'Oh Lord, the great and terrible God, who keeps covenant and steadfast love with those who love him and keep his commandments'" (Dan. 9:4).

Paul replaces the Law with "love": "He who loves his neighbor has fulfilled the Law" (Rom. 13:8-10; Jas. 2:8). This is not new to Jews: Rabbi Akibah said that the commandment, "You shall love your neighbor as yourself" (Lev. 19:18), is the great principle of the Torah. For Paul, fulfilling the Law is "completing and dispensing with it." For the Jew, it is understanding and practicing its essence and *preserving* it!

FOR ISRAEL THE LAW WAS LIFE

For Paul the Law is slavery and death: "The written code kills, but the spirit gives life" (Rom. 8:2; II Cor. 3:6). For Israel, it is life: "You shall therefore keep my statutes and my ordinances, by doing which a man shall live" (Lev. 18:5; Neh. 9:29; Ezek. 20:11,13,21) "Be careful to do all the words of this law. For it is no trifle for you, but it is your life" (Deut. 32:46,47; 30:6,8; 5:33). "If the law had not been my delight, I should have perished...I will never forget your precepts for by them have you given me life" (Ps. 119:92,93). "My son, forget not my teaching, but let your heart keep my commandments; for length of days and years of life and abundant welfare will they give you" (Prov. 3:1,2). For Paul, "the Law made nothing perfect" (Heb. 7:19); but for the Psalmist, "The law of YHVH is perfect, reviving the soul..." (Ps. 19:7):A "perfect" law need not be abrogated. The reward for keeping the Law was life in abundance (Lev. 25:18; 26:3-12; Deut. 4:l; Prov. 3:18).

PAUL'S MISUNDERSTANDING OF "THE RIGHTEOUS SHALL LIVE BY FAITH"

Paul says: "Now it is evident that no man is justified before God by the law; for 'The righteous shall live by faith.' And the law is not of faith; but, 'The man that does them shall live in them'" (Gal. 3:11,12; Hab. 2:4). The Hebrew of Paul's quotation from Habakkuk is, *Tsadik be-emunato yichyeh.* Paul misapprehends the words of Habakkuk. The full quote is: "Behold, he whose soul is not upright [*yashar*] is puffed up; but the righteous shall live in his faithfulness." The Hebrew *emunah* here does not mean *Faith* in the Christian sense of belief, but "faithfulness, integrity, loyalty": "Moses' hands...were steady [*emunah*) (Exod. 17:12); "Of Moses it is written: "A man faithful [*ne-e-man*] in all my house" (Num. 12:7). In II Ki. 12:15 (H,16), *emunah* refers to the honesty of the money-keepers. In Prov. 20:6, "Most men will proclaim every one his good works; but a faithful man [*ish-emunim*], who can find"? *Ne-eman* does not mean "having faith," or "believing," but "faithful," "trustworthy," "loyal". God is called *El Emunah*, "God of Faithfulness." In Ps. 96:13, the synonym of faithfulness (*emunah*) is justice. A correct understanding, then, of Hab. 2:4 is: The righteous are rewarded with [long] life because of their integrity.

In quoting Habakkuk 2:4, Paul contradicts himself. Paul teaches that the Law is death-dealing, whereas Habakkuk holds out life for faithful observance of the Law. This is not a vain hope. It would not have been offered were it an impossibility.

But is not the above contradicted by Ps. 143:2: "Enter not into judgment with your servant; for no man living is righteous before you..."? We are not condemned because we are fallible: "If you, YHVH, should mark iniquities, Lord, who could stand? But there is forgiveness with you" (Ps. 130:3,4). Thus, the Psalmist dispenses with the whole scheme of Christian atonement. Because there is no condemnation, "justification" is unnecessary

WHY THE LAW?

Paul misunderstands the purpose of the Law. It was not intended to "justify" man before God but make him holy (Exod. 22:31; Lev. 11:43,44). Indeed, when a Jew performs a ritual commandment, he blesses God "who has sanctified us by his commandments."

"THE COMMANDMENT IS NOT TOO HARD FOR YOU"

Paul said: "All who rely on works of the law are under a curse, as it is written, 'Cursed be every one who does not keep all the things written in the book of the law, to do them'" (Gal. 3:10-13). Paul is quoting Deut. 27:26: "Cursed be he who does not confirm the words of this law by doing them." (CF Deut. 28:15). Paul's meaning is that those under the Law Covenant are cursed, being unable to keep the *entire* law. This distorts Moses' teaching. We are not expected to keep the law "perfectly." The highest standard—performing *all* the commandments—is set before us, although it is understood that imperfect man cannot observe the entire Law: "You shall remember and do *all* my commandments, and be holy to your God" (Num. 15:40). God tells Abraham, "Walk before me and be *perfect*" (Gen.

17:1; cf. Lev. 26:3). We *strive* for perfection and the imitation of God's holiness although we often fail (Lev. 19:2): "You are not obligated to complete the work; but neither are you free to desist from it" (Aboth 2:16). Paul's assumption that a perfect law was given to convict imperfect man is erroneous. The One who fashioned us knows our limitations and does not demand perfection: "As a father pities his children, so YHVH pities those who fear him. For he knows our frame; he remembers that we are dust" (Ps. 103:14). God requires only our sincere endeavor: "Do *with your might* what your hands find to do" (Eccl. 9:10).

"CHOOSE LIFE!"

Those under the Law have a choice of life or death: "I have set before you life and death, blessing and curse; therefore choose life, that you and your descendants may live" (Deut. 30:19). The Law was reasonable: "For this commandment which I command you this day is not too hard for you, neither is it far off...But the word is very near you; it is in your mouth and in your heart, so that *you can do it*" (Deut. 30:11-14). Compare this optimistic view with the pessimism of Paul: "For I know that nothing good dwells within me, that is, in my flesh. I can will what is right, but I cannot do it. For I do not do the good I want, but the evil I do not want is what I do" (Rom. 7:18-20). Contrast Paul's pessimism with God's admonition to Cain: "Sin is couching at the door; its desire is for you, but *you can master* it" (Gen. 4:7).

"BLESSED IS HE WHOSE TRANSGRESSION IS FORGIVEN"

Deuteronomy 28 contains curses for breaking the law, but also *blessings* for keeping it. Paul refers to the *curses* but omits the blessings! The curses are not irrevocable; repentance annuls them: "If they confess their iniquity...and make amends...then I will remember my covenant..." (Lev. 26:40–45). "And when all these things come upon you, the blessing and the curse, which I have set before you, and you call them to mind...and return to YHVH your God...then YHVH your God will restore your fortunes, and have compassion upon you..." (Deut. 30:1—3; See also Ps. 32:1,5; Prov. 28:13; Isa. l:16–18; 55:7).

"JUSTIFIED BY FAITH APART FROM WORKS OF LAW"—PAUL

Arguing for justification by faith not law, Paul says: "A man is justified by faith apart from works of law...For if Abraham was justified by works, he has something to boast about, but not before God. For what does the scripture say? 'Abraham believed God and it was reckoned to him as righteousness...'" (Rom. 3:28–4:3). Paul argues incorrectly that Abraham's justification was independent of Torah-keeping. Abraham the "prophet" (Gen. 20:7) kept the "pre-Torah": "Abraham obeyed my voice and kept my charge, my commandments, my statutes, and my laws (*torotai*)" (Gen. 26:5). Indeed, the Torah *preceded* Sinai (Exod. 15:26; 16:4,28; 18:16).

"YOU REPAY A MAN ACCORDING TO HIS WORK"—JAMES

James said: "Was not Abraham our father justified by works, when he offered his son Isaac upon the altar?…'Abraham believed God, and it was reckoned to him as righteousness'" (Jas. 2:21–23; Gen. 15:6; 26:5). This contradicts Paul's statement that "No human being will be justified in his sight by works of the law" (Rom. 3:20,28; 4:2; 11:6; Gal. 2:16; 3:10; Eph. 2:8,9; II Tim. 1:9). Keeping the Law brings righteousness: "And it will be righteousness for us if we carefully observe this commandment" (Deut. 6:25; 24:10–13). "In his righteousness which he has done, he shall live" (Ezek. 18:21,22). We are judged by *deeds*: "For YHVH is righteous, he loves righteous deeds; the upright shall behold his face" (Ps. 11:7; 18:20–24, 62:12; 112:1,5,6,9; Pr. 24:12; Isa. 3:10; 64:5; Jer. 17:10; 32:19; Ezek. 18:30; Mt. 5:16; Rom. 2:6). "YHVH, who shall sojourn in your tent? Who shall dwell on your holy hill? He who walks blamelessly, and does what is right…" (Ps. 15:l—5; 24:3–5; 34:11-16; Isa. 58:6–14; Mal. 3:5; Acts 10:35). "He has showed you, O man, what is good; and what YHVH requires of you, but to do justice, and to love kindness, and to walk humbly with your God" (Mic. 6:8). "Fear God, and keep his commandments; for this is the whole duty of man" (Eccl. 11:13,14).

"A RIGHTEOUS MAN FALLS SEVEN TIMES"

Paul says: "It is written, 'There is none righteous, no, not one'…All have sinned, and come short of the glory of God" (Rom. 3:10,23). Paul is misquoting Ps. 14:3, "There is none that does good, no, not one." This certainly does not mean that *all* are evil—only those who *deny* God are meant (v. 1). The next Psalm speaks of those who are "blameless." There *are* righteous and good men: "Surely there is not a righteous man on earth who does good and never sins" (Eccl. 7:20): His sin does not of necessity render him evil. This is different from saying, "There are no *sinless* men. In the eyes of God, righteousness does not demand sinlessness: A righteous man falls seven times, and rises again…" (Prov. 24:16). "The eyes of YHVH are toward the righteous" (Ps. 34:15 [16]). "A righteous man who walks in his integrity—blessed are his children after him" (Prov. 20:7). "Who shall ascend the hill of YHVH? He who has clean hands and pure heart, who does not lift up his soul to what is false, and does not swear deceitfully. He will receive blessing from YHVH, and vindication from the God of his salvation" (Ps. 24:3–5). It *is* possible to have clean hands and a pure heart"! Intentions are important:; "YHVH looks upon the heart" (I Sam. 16:7). The Creator is not implacable but forgoes anger. He understands our imperfect nature and is compassionate toward those into whom He breathed life: "I will not contend forever, nor will I always be angry; for from me proceeds the spirit, and I have made the breath of life" (Isa. 57:15,16). Repentance brings forgiveness: "If they sin against you—for there is none that does not sin—if they repent with all their mind and with all their heart...hear thou in heaven...and forgive your people" (I Ki. 8:46-53).

EXAMPLES OF "RIGHTEOUS" INDIVIDUALS

Scripture mentions various "righteous" individuals: "*Enoch* walked with God" (Gen. 5:22); "*Noah* was a righteous man, blameless in his generation" (Gen. 6:9; 7:1); "[Abraham] believed YHVH; and he reckoned it to him as righteousness" (Gen. 15:6; 17:1); "[Job] was blameless and upright, one who feared God, and turned away from evil" (Job 1:1,8); *David* said, "Preserve my soul for I am godly" (Ps. 86:2); David walked before God "in purity of heart and uprightness" (I Ki. 9:4); *Hezekiah* walked before God "in truth and with a perfect heart" (II Ki. 20:3). *Zechariah* and *Elizabeth* were "righteous before God, walking in the commandments and ordinances of the Lord, blameless" (Lu. 1:5,6). Yet, remarkably, Paul said, "The law made nothing perfect" (Heb. 7:18,19)!

"OUR RIGHTEOUSNESS IS AS FILTHY RAGS"

How, then, are we to understand Isaiah: "All our righteousness is as filthy rags" (Isa. 64:5)? This refers to self-righteousness—religious works done for personal glory. And what of Job: "Who can bring a clean thing out of an unclean thing?" (Job 14:4; 15:14,15; 25:4)? Job uttered these words in his despondency, including even the angels, stars and moon in his cynicism! His words are not a universal indictment of humanity but should be balanced against the optimistic assessment of man's potential, expressed throughout Scripture.

PAUL: THE LAW AROUSES SINFUL PASSIONS

Paul blames the Law for "arousing his sinful passions": "While we were living in the flesh, our sinful passions, aroused by the law, were at work in our members to bear fruit for death...What shall we say then? That the law is sin? By no means! For if it had not been for the law, I should not have known sin I should not have known what it is to covet if the law had not said, 'You shall not covet.' But sin, finding opportunity in the commandment, wrought in me all kinds of covetousness...So the law is holy, and the commandment is holy and just and good..." (Rom. 7:5–11). Paul contradicts himself: First he praises the Law as being holy, just and good; then he blames the Law for arousing sinful passions. Does Paul wish a society free from law? Would Paul blame God for Adam and Eve's sin because God issued the prohibition? Did the ambition awaken the desire to eat the forbidden fruit? Then why punish them? What provoked Cain to slay his brother? There was no law prohibiting murder! They sinned by yielding to a natural human inclination. Paul should not fault the Law for his own weaknesses.

Unlike Paul, the Psalmist did not think the Law "incited to sin": "The law of YHVH is perfect…the commandment of YHVH is pure…By them is your servant warned; in keeping them there is great reward" (Ps. 19:7–13). How much saner and wiser is the Psalmist's understanding.

NO SEPARATION BETWEEN "CEREMONIAL" AND "MORAL" LAW

According to Christian teaching, the "ceremonial law," not the "moral law," was abrogated." Paul makes no such distinction. He blames the commandment, "You shall not covet"—a *moral* commandment—for inciting sin! Discarding a *part* of the Law violates what Israel was taught: "Everything I command you, you shall be careful to do; you shall not add to it or take away from it" (Deut. 12:32 [H. 13:1]).

PAUL SUBSTITUTES NEW LAWS FOR OLD

Paul would abrogate the Mosaic Law—but not *LAW*! Indeed, the Christian Scriptures contain many laws: "Do you not know that the unrighteous will not inherit the kingdom of God? Do not be deceived; neither the immoral, nor idolaters, nor adulterers, nor homosexuals, nor thieves, nor the greedy, nor drunkards, nor revilers, nor robbers…" (I Cor. 6:9,10; cf. also Gal. 5:20,21; Eph. 4:25–32; 5:3–5; 6:1,2; Col. 3:5–9,18–22; I Tim. 3:l—13; ch. 5; Tit. 2:1–10; Jas. 1:27; 5:12). Holding Paul to his argument—by mentioning idolatry, adultery, homosexuality, theft, greed and drunkenness, is Paul inciting to sin"? Jesus criticized the Pharisees and Scribes for imposing insuperable burdens on the people (Mt. 23:4); but he himself made difficult demands: "He that is angry with his brother without a cause shall be liable to judgment…He that says 'You fool!' shall be liable to hell fire…He that looks lustfully at a woman has already committed adultery with her…Love your enemies…Do not accumulate wealth…Judge not that you be not judged" (Mt. 5:21,27,28,43;6:19;7:1–5). Jesus even advocates self-castration to subdue sexual desire (Mt. 19:12)! In mentioning the sins of uncontrolled anger, lustfulness, avarice and prejudice, is Jesus 'inciting the commission of these sins'?

LOVE NOT A DEPENDABLE MOTIVATION FOR DUTY

Humanity must have law: "The heart is deceitful" (Jer. 17:9). Man is fickle and self-willed. Love cannot always be relied upon to summon to duty. Duty must be performed even if unpleasant—even though love may be absent. It is not always pleasant to visit the sick, care for the aged, rear recalcitrant children, bury the dead, perform justice to an enemy. Laws are needed for decisive action when we are debating with our emotions. For example: "If you meet your enemy's ox or his ass going astray, you shall bring it back to him. If you see the ass of one who hates you lying under its burden, you shall refrain from leaving him with it, you shall help him lift it up" (Exod. 23:4,5). Not love, but justice and obedience to Law, would impel this behavior toward an enemy. Whereas Jesus would have us "love our enemies," the Law requires only that we treat them justly.

The Talmud teaches: "Greater is he who is commanded and acts than he who acts without being commanded" (Kid. 31a). The Rabbis understood human nature well. Instinct cannot always be depended upon to propel us to right behavior and the performance of deeds of lovingkindness. Rules are constant, emotions transient.

BRIT HACHADASHAH—NEW TESTAMENT (COVENANT)

Hebrew Christians speak of the *Brit Hachadashah*, the "New Covenant." This has a dual meaning: (1) The new Christian dispensation, in which "grace" replaces "law"; (2) The Christian Scriptures—the "Book of the New Covenant." In Christian theology, the "New Covenant" replaces the "Old" Covenant: "[Jesus] abolishes the first in order to establish the second" (Heb. 10:9). "Therefore he is the mediator of a new covenant, so that those who are called may receive the promised eternal inheritance, since a death has occurred which redeems them from the transgressions under the first covenant" (Heb. 9:15,16). "If that first covenant had been faultless, there would have been no occasion for a second... What is becoming obsolete and growing old is ready to vanish" (Heb. 8:7,13).

MEANING OF "NEW COVENANT" IN JER. 31:31-34

To support the abolition of the "old Law covenant," Paul quotes Jeremiah: "Behold, the days are coming, says YHVH, when I will make a new covenant with the house of Israel and the house of Judah not like the covenant which I made with their fathers when I took them by the hand to bring them out of the land of Egypt, my covenant which they broke, though I was their husband, says YHVH. But this is the covenant which I will make with the house of Israel after those days, says YHVH: I will put my law within them, and I will write it upon their hearts; and I will be their God, and they shall be my people. And no longer shall each man teach his neighbor and each his brother, saying, 'Know YHVH,' for they shall all know me, from the least of them to the greatest, says YHVH; for I will forgive their iniquity, and I will remember their sin no more" (31:31–34).

In his quotation, Paul takes no account of what follows Jeremiah's words, namely, God's promise that the "descendants of Israel" will be as eternal as the heavens and the earth (vv. 35–37). Paul misapprehends the Jeremiah prophecy. For Paul, the Law Covenant is superseded by a new covenant, enacted with the Gentiles. This is not the case. The Covenant is with "*the house of Israel and the house of Judah*," not with the Church! The Law Covenant was eternal, never to be abrogated: "Nor is it with you only that I make this sworn covenant, but with him who is not here with us this day...*our children forever*" (Deut. 29:14,29). "He established a testimony in Jacob, and appointed a law in Israel, which he commanded our fathers to teach to their children; that the next generation might know them, the children yet unborn, and arise and tell them to their children, so that they should set their hope in God, and forget not the works of God, but keep his commandments" (Ps. 78:5–7; cf. Ps. 103:17,18; Gen. 17:9–14; Exod. 27:21; 31:16, 17; Lev. 24:8; Deut. 12:28; Est. 9:28; Ps. 111:5–9; Isa. 59:21). A teacher in Israel who forgets the Law is severely censured: "My people are destroyed for lack of knowledge. Because you have rejected knowledge, I shall reject you from being a priest to me. Since you have forgotten the Torah of your God, I, for my part, will forget your children" (Hos. 4:6).

Those who deny that the Law Covenant is "eternal" argue that "eternal" (*olam*) means, "for a time undisclosed." We reply with Gen. 21:33: "Abraham...called upon the name of YHVH, the Everlasting God (*El Olam*)." Is there any ambiguity regarding the meaning of *Olam*—eternal—as applied to God? "The steadfast love of YHVH is from everlasting to everlasting...to those who keep his covenant and remember to do his commandments" (Ps. 103:17,18). No suggestion here of any "Torah-abrogation."

In the Jeremiah passage quoted above, the Law covenant is not replaced but *reaffirmed*, as was done by King Josiah: "And the king made a covenant before YHVH, to walk after YHVH and to keep his commandments and his testimonies and his statutes, *with all his heart and all his soul*...(II Ki. 23:1–3). Josiah was not making a *new* covenant but *reaffirming* the existing covenant (cf. Lev. 26:40-45). Jeremiah is not speaking of the Torah's replacement but of a *renewed relationship* between the People Israel and the Covenant.

Writing the law "on the heart" signifies willing obedience and renewed dedication to the *Law*: "YHVH your God will circumcise your heart and the heart of your offspring so that you will love YHVH your God with all your heart and with all your soul, that you may live...and you shall again obey the voice of YHVH, and keep all his commandments" (Deut. 30:6,8). "A new heart I will give you…And I will put my spirit within you, and cause you to walk in my statutes and be careful to observe my ordinances" (Ezek. 36:26,27; 11:19,20; 16:60). It should not be overlooked that the Law as first given to Israel was to be *upon the heart*: "And these words which I command you this day shall be upon your heart" (Deut. 6:6). David said: "I delight to do your will, O my God; your law is within my heart" (Ps. 40:8). Isaiah expresses a similar sentiment: "Hearken to me, you who know righteousness, the people in whose heart is my Torah" (Isa. 51:7).

Jeremiah said that with the renewal of the covenant "they shall all know me." Did Jesus' coming result in the universal knowledge of God? Jeremiah said, "I will forgive their iniquity and I will remember their sin no more." Did Jesus' coming bring forgiveness to Israel? In Jeremiah 31, God is the focus; there is no suggestion of any "christology"! Forgiveness is freely given, without a required "sin offering" (cf. Hos. 14:4)!

LAW OBSERVED IN MESSIANIC TIMES

In Messianic times, the Mosaic Law is universally observed: "Remember the law of my servant Moses, the statutes and ordinances that I commanded him at Horeb for all Israel. Behold, I will send you Elijah the prophet before the great and terrible day of YHVH comes" (Mal. 4:4,5). "My servant David shall be king over them…and they shall walk in my ordinances and observe and perform my statutes" (Ezek. 37:24). "Out of Zion shall go forth the Law…" (Isa. 2:3). "From new moon to new moon, and from Sabbath to Sabbath, all flesh shall come to worship before me, says YHVH" (Isa. 66:23; cf. Ps. 89:27–32; Zech. 14:16). Messiah is foreshadowed by the high priest Levi, of whom God says: "My covenant was with him for *life and for peace*…for the lips of a priest should guard knowledge and *they should seek Torah from his mouth*, for he is the messenger of YHVH of hosts" (Mal. 2:5-8). The Law Covenant made with Israel and administered by the priestly class Levi meant *life* and *peace* for Israel and was to endure *for life*!

The Covenant's renewal is marked by universal knowledge of God: "No longer shall each man teach his neighbor and each his brother, saying, 'Know YHVH,' for they shall all know me." (v. 34). If, as Paul claims, the "New Covenant" was made with Christians, where now is the promised *universal* knowledge of God?

THE LAW, AN ETERNAL SIGN BETWEEN GOD AND ISRAEL

The following Scriptural summary demonstrates the conflict between Judaism and Christianity regarding the Law: ["CS"=Christian Scriptures; "HS"=Hebrew Scriptures.]

(CS)   "Christ is the end of the law" (Rom. 10:4). "[He abolished] in his flesh the law of commandments and ordinances" (Eph. 2:15). "You are not under the law but under grace" (Rom. 6:14).

(HS)   "He has commanded his covenant forever' (Ps. 111:9). "It is a sign forever between me and the children of Israel" (Exod. 31:16,17).

(CS)   "The written code kills" (2 Cor. 3:6). "The commandment which was ordained to life, I found to be death to me" (Rom. 7:10).

(HS)   "You shall therefore keep my statutes and my ordinances, by doing which a man shall live" (Lev. 18:5). "Length of days, years of life and abundant welfare will they give you...It is a tree of life to those who hold fast to it" (Prov. 3:1,2,18).

(CS)   "Christ redeemed us from the curse of the law" (Gal. 3:10,13).

(HS)   "I have set before you life and death, blessing and curse; therefore choose life" (Deut. 30:19).

(CS)   "The law made nothing perfect" (Heb. 7:19; Rom. 3:20; Gal. 2:16; Eph. 2:8).

(HS)   "The law of YHVH is perfect" (Ps. 19:7). "It will be righteousness for us if we are careful to do all the commandments" (Deut. 6:25). "The just man falls seven times and rises" (Prov. 24:16). "You reward a man according to his works" (Ps. 62:12; Jer. 17:10). "Job was blameless and upright" (Job 1:1,8). "The commandment...is not too hard for you" (Deut. 30:11).

(CS)   "Why do you tempt God, to put a yoke upon the neck of the disciples, which neither our fathers nor we are able to bear?" (Acts 15:10; Gal. 5:1).

(HS)   "I will keep your law...I shall walk at liberty . I love your law...Your word is a lamp to my feet and a light to my path" (Ps. 119:45,97,105; Deut. 10:12,13; 13:3,4). "What great nation is there that has statutes and ordinances so righteous as all this law which I set before you this day!" (Deut. 4:8). "YHVH was pleased, for his righteousness sake, to magnify his law and make it glorious" (Isa. 42:21).

             *   *   *

    The Talmud comments on Jer. 16:11, "[They] have forsaken me and not kept My law.": "Would that they had forsaken Me but kept My law" (Haggigah 1:7).

CHAPTER 14

SATAN: REAL FOR CHRISTIANS

"Messianic Jews," together with most Christians, believe in the existence of Satan the Devil, regarding him as the arch-tempter, the cause of all evil. For them he is a living, ever-present, powerful spirit being with whom believers must contend: "We wrestle not against flesh and blood, but against principalities, against powers, against the rulers of the darkness of this world, against wicked spirits in heavenly places" (Eph. 6:11,12; 2:2). "The god of this world has blinded the minds of them which believe not" (II Cor. 4:4; 2:11; I Jn. 5:19). "Be sober, be vigilant, for your adversary the devil, as a roaring lion, walks about seeking whom he may devour" (I Pet. 5:8; Jas. 4:7).

"GOD WILL SOON CRUSH SATAN"

Paul said Jesus died "to destroy him who has the power of death, that is, the devil" (Heb. 2:14). He declared Satan's end was imminent: "The God of peace will soon crush Satan under your feet" (Rom. 16:20). Yet evil and death still prevail! Did Paul think "soon" meant thousands of years in the future? Jesus likewise preached that Satan's end was near: "*Now* is the judgment of this world; *now* shall the prince of this world be cast out…" (Jn. 12:31; cf. Rev. 12:12). What did he mean by now and by the 'casting out of the prince of this world'? Did it signify the end of the rule of wickedness? If so, wickedness still reigns!

"YOU SHALL BRUISE HIS HEEL"

Christians interpret Gen. 3:15 as predicting the end of Satan at the hands of the Messiah: "I will put enmity between you and the woman, and between your seed and her seed; he shall bruise your head, and you shall bruise his heel."— Satan was to "bruise the heel" of Jesus—not a mortal wound; Jesus was to bruise the head of Satan—a mortal wound. By his death, therefore, Jesus was to vanquish Satan. Do Christians believe he did? Are not the wounding of the seed— Jesus' death—and the crushing of the serpent simultaneous? Was not Jesus' death, therefore, to be followed by the cessation of evil?

SO-CALLED ALLUSIONS TO SATAN

There are six possible allusions to Satan in the Hebrew Scriptures; upwards of fifty in the Christian Scriptures. In the Garden of Eden (Gen. 3), the serpent is not a spirit being but a "creature of the field." Yes, it talks; but so did Balaam's ass (Num. 22:28–30). In Job, Satan is not God's rival but only one of God's recalcitrant "sons" (Job 1:6). He has no power or authority except by God's permission; and the contest concerns only Job, not mankind. By contrast, Satan of the Christian Scriptures is "the god of this world" (II Cor. 4:4).

"YOU CAN OVERCOME IT!"

For Jews, Satan was never more than a figure of folklore. For Christians, Satan is a reality. The Jew does not wrestle with wicked spirits in heavenly places—a melancholy thought! The specter of a powerful spirit being, ever seeking to ensnare us, is religious paranoia. It is much saner to attribute our problems to our own doing. It is more humane and hopeful to struggle with our own weaknesses than with some evil, supernatural power. When a Jew commits a wrong, he does not blame "evil forces" but his own shortcomings. Jews are not hounded by the image of an unseen, malevolent spirit-adversary who constantly besets our path, seeking opportunities to tempt us to evil. For Jews, temptation comes from within *ourselves* and it is within *our power* to overcome it. Indeed, we *do* wrestle with flesh and blood' (our own) and not with wicked spirits. When Cain was downcast over the rejection of his offering, God said to him: "If you do well, will you not be accepted? But if you do not do well, sin is couching at the door; its desire is for you, but you can rule over it" (Gen. 4:7). David prayed: "Let not sin rule over me" (Ps. 119:133). Sin couches at the door of our hearts. The "deceiver," is not Satan but our own emotions and psyche (Jer. 17:9). We have the power to overcome sin: "Wash yourselves; make yourselves clean…though your sins be as scarlet, they shall be as white as snow; though they be red like crimson, they shall be as wool"

(Isa. 1:16–18). The initiative is ours. Man, whom God has made a little lower than the angels (Ps. 8:5), has the responsibility and the capability to improve *himself.* He need only be guided by the wisdom of Torah (teaching): "The Torah of YHVH is perfect, reviving the soul…by them is your servant warned" (Ps. 19:7–13). "It is a tree of life to those who lay hold of her" (Prov. 3:18).

"I, YHVH, MAKE PEACE AND CREATE EVIL"

The belief in two opposing deities—God and Satan—is of pagan origin and is contrary to Israelite Monotheism. It is reminiscent of the Dualism of the ancient Persians, for whom Ormuzd was the god of good and Ahriman the god of evil. To admit of a secondary power of evil in the world is to deny the one God: "Whom have I in heaven but you" (Ps. 73:25)? God is the source of all—good *and* evil: "There is none beside me; I am YHVH and there is no other. I form light and create darkness, I make peace and create evil. I YHVH do all these" (Isa. 45:6,7). "There is no god with me. I cause death and give life" (Deut. 32:39). "Shall we receive good at the hand of God, and shall we not receive evil?" (Job 2:10). Pure Monotheism does not allow for a Devil-Tempter.

CHAPTER 15

THE "END" AND THE "SECOND COMING"

"THE KINGDOM IS AT HAND!"

In the world of commerce, an unfailing device for attracting shoppers is the advertisement, "Closing our doors forever!" This also works well in the world of religion. Religious groups proclaim the imminent "End of the World," set dates, and the faithful wait hopefully for their redemption. When the promised End fails to materialize, the figures and data are re-examined, "errors" in calculation are discovered, and new projections are made. The faithful continue to hope.

The early Christians likewise expected the End. John the Baptist preached: "Repent, for the kingdom of heaven is at *hand*...I baptize you with water for repentance, but he who is coming after me...will baptize you with the holy spirit and with fire. His winnowing fork is in his hand, and he will clear his threshing floor and gather his wheat into the granary, but the chaff he will burn with unquenchable fire" (Mt. 3:1,2,11,12). John's words convey finality—total consummation! Jesus also proclaimed the End: "Repent, for the kingdom of heaven is at hand" (Mt. 4:17; 10:7; Mk. 1:15). For those who disdained his message, Jesus warned: "It shall be more tolerable for the land of Sodom and Gomorrah in the day of judgment than for that city" (Mt. 10:15; Lu. 10:8-12). The "day of judgment" was imminent!

Jesus proclaimed: "The Son of man is to come with his angels in the glory of his Father, and then he will repay every man for what he has done. Truly, I say to you, there are some standing here who will not taste death before they see the Son of man coming in his kingdom" (Mt. 16:27,28; Mk. 8:38; 9:1; Lu. 9:26,27): In the lifetime of his listeners, Jesus would make a glorious appearance with his angels to execute judgment. Clearly, the End was expected *then*!

The Christian Scriptures are replete with references to the End: "*You* will be hated by all for my name's sake but he who endures to the end will be saved…You will not have gone through all of the towns of Israel before the Son of man comes" (Mt. 10:22,23). Jesus was not addressing some imaginary followers in the twentieth century; he was speaking to his followers in the *first* century, announcing the end of that age and the hope of salvation.

"THIS GENERATION SHALL NOT PASS AWAY TILL ALL THESE THINGS ARE FULFILLED"

"As [Jesus] sat on the mount of Olives, the disciples came to him privately, saying, 'Tell us, when will this be, and what will be the sign of your coming and the end of the world?'" After enumerating a number of signs, Jesus continues: "'He that endures to the end will be saved. And this gospel of the kingdom will be preached throughout the whole world, as a testimony to all nations; and then the end will come'" (Mt. 24:3–14). Jesus then describes the critical times that will precede the End and says: "'Unless those days were shortened, no flesh would be saved; but for the elect's sake those days will be shortened…This generation will not pass away till all these things are fulfilled'" (Mt 24:22,34; Mk. 13:30; Lu. 21:32). Clearly, Jesus meant the End would come in *their* time.

"Jehovah's Witnesses," who preach that the End will come in our time, have given Jesus words an ingenious twist: The wars and calamities which Jesus predicted began to occur only after 1914. The "generation" living at that time would live to see the final consummation of events predicted by Jesus. But these End-preachers face a problem: The "generation" of 1914 is reaching an advanced age and *will* soon pass away! But not to worry—new and ingenious interpretations will be devised to satisfy the faithful.

"YOU MUST BE READY!"

Jesus urged his followers to prepare for the kingdom: "Fear not, little flock, for it is your Father's good pleasure to give you the kingdom. Sell your possessions…Be like men who are waiting for their master to come home from the marriage feast…Be ready; for the Son of man is coming at an hour you do not expect" (Lu. 12:32–40). While some religious devotees have been known to sell their possessions in anticipation of the End, this has not yet occurred among the

Jehovah's Witnesses. Although they preach the End, they do not appear to take it seriously enough to divest themselves of their possessions!

We would ask the "End-preachers": Since Jesus said, "All power is given to me in heaven and in earth" (Mt. 28:18), why was it necessary to wait until the twentieth century for the millennium? When Jesus said, "Fear not, little flock, for it is your Father's good pleasure to give you the kingdom," *what* "little flock" did he mean and *when* would they receive the kingdom? Of course, the twentieth-century "millennialists" think *they* are the "little flock" and the kingdom will come in *their* generation!

"NOW IS THE JUDGMENT OF THIS WORLD!"

In anticipation of his impending death, Jesus said: "Now is the judgment of this world, now shall the ruler of this world be cast out; and I, when I am lifted up from the earth, will draw all men to myself..." (Jn. 12:31–33; 16:11; cf. Heb. 2:14). Jesus predicted the *imminent* judgment of the world, debasement of Satan (Lu. 10:18; II Cor. 4:4; Eph 2:2), and conversion of all mankind. All these events were to occur in *his* day. None of them did! Although Jesus came to destroy the works of the devil" (I Jn. 3:8), evil still prevails. The Christian Scriptures unequivocally predicted the Devil's demise *then*, not several millennia later.

Jesus said: "The hour is coming, and *now* is, when the dead shall hear the voice of the Son of God; and they that hear shall live...All that are in the graves shall hear his voice, and shall come forth" (Jn. 5:25,29). Jesus' language conveys immediacy; the universal resurrection of the dead was imminent. His prophecy, however, failed of fulfillment!

"THE END OF ALL THINGS IS AT HAND!"

Repeatedly, down through the ages and in modern times, religious groups have prophesied the coming of the End and have projected dates "End-prophesying" is revived in every generation, while the patience of the faithful never seems to be exhausted. In early Christian times, when the End-prophecy of Jesus did not materialize, Christian hope never faltered. Paul continues to refer to the End: "He has fixed a day in which he will judge the world" (Acts 17:31). "I consider that the sufferings of this present time are not worth comparing with the glory that is to be revealed to us. For the creation waits with eager longing for the revealing of the sons of God...we groan inwardly as we wait for adoption as sons, the redemption of our bodies...we wait for it with patience" (Rom. 8:18–25).

"THE NIGHT IS FAR GONE, THE DAY IS AT HAND"

Modern prophesiers of the End may transpose Paul's words to the twentieth century; but it is clear Paul sought for the End in *his immediate future*: "Besides this you know what hour it is, how it is full time now for you to wake from sleep. For salvation is nearer to us now than when we first believed; the night is far gone, the day is at hand" (Rom. 13:11,12). "The God of peace will soon crush Satan under your feet" (Rom. 16:20). "The appointed time has grown very short…The form of this world is passing away" (I Cor. 7:29,31). "All these things happened to them for examples and are written for our admonition, upon whom the End of the world is come" (I Cor. 10:11). "We shall not all sleep, but we shall be changed" (I Cor. 15:51). "Our Lord, come!" (I Cor. 16:22). Now is the acceptable time; behold, now is the day of salvation" (II Cor. 6:2). "Grace to you and peace from God the Father and our Lord Jesus Christ, who gave himself for our sins to deliver us from the *present* evil world" (Gal. 1:4). "He who began a good work in you will bring it to completion at the day of Jesus Christ" (Php. 1:6). "Our commonwealth is in heaven, and from it we await a Savior, the Lord Jesus Christ, who will change our lowly body to be like his glorious body" (Php. 3:20). (Paul is not speaking of resurrection for believers at death and continuing for all time. He is referring to a sudden change to a spiritual body [Cf. Jn. 5:25,29; Rom. 8:23; I Thess. 4:17].) "The Lord is at hand" (Php. 4:5). "When Christ who is our life appears, then you also will appear with him in glory" (Col. 3:4)"…To wait for his Son from heaven" (I Thess. 1:10). "We who are alive, who are left until the coming of the Lord, shall not precede those who have fallen asleep…The dead in Christ will rise first; then we who are alive, who are left, shall be caught up together with them in the clouds to meet the Lord in the air…" (I Thess. 4:13–18). "…until the appearing of our Lord Jesus Christ" (I Tim. 6:14). "…in these last days he has spoken to us by a Son" (Heb. 1:2). "We share in Christ if only we hold our first confidence firm to the end" (Heb. 3:14; 6:11). "…Now, once in the end of the world, he has appeared to put away sin by the sacrifice of himself…To them that look for him he shall appear the second time without sin, for salvation" (Heb. 9:26,28). "Not neglecting to meet together…all the more as you see the day drawing near…For yet a little while, and the coming one shall come and shall not tarry…" (Heb. 10:25,37).

"CHILDREN, IT IS THE LAST HOUR"

James, Peter and John also hoped for the End *in their day*: "Be patient therefore, brethren, until the coming of the Lord for the coming of the Lord *is at hand*" (Jas. 5:7,8). "…for a salvation *ready to be revealed in the last time*. In this you rejoice, though now *for a little while*…Therefore gird up your minds, be sober, set your hope fully upon the grace that is coming to you at the revelation of Jesus Christ…[Christ] was made manifest *at the end of the times* for your sake" (I Pet. 1:5,6,13,20). "The end of all things is *at hand*" (I Pet. 4:7; also II Pet. 3:3-14). "Children, it is the *last* hour" (I Jn. 2:18). "The revelation of Jesus Christ, which God gave him to show to his servants what must *soon* take place…The time is *near*…Behold, he is coming with the clouds, and every eye will see him…" (Rev. 1:1,3,7). "I am coming *soon* (Rev. 3:11). "[The Devil] knows he has but *a short time*" (Rev. 12:12). "The time is near…I am coming *soon*…Come, Lord Jesus!" (Rev. 22:10,20).

The teaching of the "Second Coming" was an innovation, necessitated by the failure of the "First Coming." When the hoped-for "Second Coming" did not materialize, it was projected to later generations.

"I WILL NEVER AGAIN CURSE THE GROUND"

In Paul's teaching of the End, nothing is said about the future of the world and its inhabitants. After the End, what happens to the planet, to humanity, to society? We hear only about believers being taken to heaven! Peter predicts the *dissolution* of the world: "The day of the Lord will come like a thief in the night; and the heavens will pass away with a loud noise, and the elements will be dissolved with fire, and the earth and the works that are upon it will be burned up" (II Pet. 3:10). But, after the flood of Noah, God promised never again to "destroy every living creature" (Gen. 8:21,22).

NO "SECOND COMING" FOR MESSIAH

The doctrine of the "End" and the "Second Coming" is flawed. Hebrew Scripture foretells the coming of the Messiah who is to redeem mankind and restore peace to the world, achieving this at his *first* and *final* coming. The notion of a "Second Coming" is not found in Hebrew Scripture. It was contrived when the Christian Messiah failed in his mission.

CHAPTER 16

MAN AND SOCIETY

"THE FLESH IS WEAK"

In the Christian Scriptures, "flesh" and "spirit," are separated, the "flesh" being denigrated as weak, lustful, sinful and vile: "The spirit indeed is willing, but the flesh is weak" (Mt. 26:41). "For I know that nothing good dwells in me, that is, in my flesh" (Rom. 7:18). "We know that our old self was crucified with him so that the sinful body might be destroyed, and we might no longer be enslaved to sin" (Rom. 6:6). who will change our lowly body to be like his glorious body" (Php. 3:21). "Those who live according to the flesh set their minds on the things of the flesh, but those who live according to the spirit set their minds on the things of the spirit" (Rom. 8:3,5). "The desires of the flesh are against the spirit, and the desires of the spirit are against the flesh; for these are opposed to each other, to prevent you from doing what you would" (Gal. 5:17).

In Christian theology, all are born with the chronic disability of sin (Rom. 5:12). "Good works" do not save; only Jesus saves: "For by grace you have been saved through faith; and this is not of your own doing, it is the gift of God—not because of works, lest any man should boast" (Eph. 2:8,9).

MAN—IN THE HEBREW SCRIPTURES

In Judaism, it is not the "flesh" that is sinful but *man*. *Man* is good or evil: "The *soul* that sins, it shall die" (Ezek. 18:4). "Carnal," meaning "evil," (Rom. 7:14; I Cor. 3:1,3) and "worldly," meaning "ungodly," (Tit. 2:12; I Jn. 2:16) are foreign to Judaism. Good works atone for sin and the antidote for sin is God's law (Prov. 3:18). Christianity emphasizes creed—"You shall believe"; Judaism emphasizes deed—"You shall do."

JUDAISM'S OPTIMISM

Judaism views man and the world optimistically: "And God saw everything he had made and behold it was very good" (Gen. 1:31). Man was created in God's image; the image was not erased because of Adam's disobedience (Gen. 9:6). "You made him little less than God and crowned him with glory and honor. You gave him dominion over the works of your hands" (Ps. 8:4–6). Man's glorious and honorable status is ongoing and was not discontinued after Eden.

"Man" in the following verse is not Adam: "God made man upright but they have sought out many inventions" (Eccl. 7:29): The Hebrew for "man" is *ha-adam*, "the man"—mankind. "*They* [plural—not just Adam but mankind] have sought out..." Mankind did not become *evil*, but, "sought out *many inventions.*" There is no suggestion of "inherited" sin. The meaning of Eccl. 7:29 is that mankind is created good but corrupts itself: "The Rock, his work is perfect...They have corrupted themselves" (Deut. 32:4,5). Each one is responsible for his own sins (Ezek. 18:20). True repentance gains forgiveness (Isa. l:16–18). "Life and death, good and evil," are in *our* hands (Deut. 30:15,16). The law is within *our* capability (Deut. 30:11-14) and is life-giving (Lev. 18:5).

ASCETICISM

In the Christian Scriptures piety is attained through suppression of "fleshly" desire and self-denial: "Walk by the spirit and do not gratify the desires of the flesh...Those who belong to Christ Jesus have crucified the flesh with its passions and desires" (Gal...5:16,24; Rom. 8:13; I Cor. 9:27; Mt. 16:24; Mk. 8:34; Lu. 9:23). "Whoever of you that does not forsake all that he has cannot be my disciple" (Lu. 14:33). "He who hates his life in this world will keep it for eternal life" (Jn. 12:25). Jesus even advocates self-castration to overcome sexual desire (Mt. 19:12)!

In Judaism asceticism does not equal piety. The Hebrew for "pious" is *chasid*, "man of lovingkindness." A saintly person is a *tsadik*, a "righteous person." The emphasis is not on a vague feeling of holiness but on *deeds of lovingkindness.* To be "religious" or "pious" is to practice justice and lovingkindness *(chesed)* (Mic. 6:8). Judaism emphasizes the deed: "Not study but deed is the essential thing" (*Aboth* 1:17). The "pious ignoramus" is alien to Judaism: "One devoid of knowledge cannot be sin-fearing; an ignoramus cannot be pious" (*Aboth* 2:45).

Judaism discourages extremes of piety: "Be not righteous to excess" (Eccl. 7:16). Saintliness is not killing desire or repressing natural instincts; we serve

God with *all* our biological drives (Deut. 6:5). Religion should enhance not impede life (Lev. 18:5; Deut. 30:11). Self-neglect is a sin, health-care a divine obligation. The Torah contains extensive health-regulations, tying them to holiness: "You shall therefore make a distinction between the clean beast and the unclean, between the clean bird and the unclean; you shall not make yourselves abominable by beast or by bird or by any thing with which the ground teems, which I have set apart for you to hold unclean. You shall be holy to me; for I YHVH am holy and have separated you from the peoples, that you should be mine" (Lev. 20:25,26; 11:44,45).

POVERTY AND WEALTH

Because the world was ending, Christians were not to accumulate wealth (Mt. 6:19; 19:23,24; Mk. 10:21; Lu. 6:20,24; 12:33). Judaism, however, neither deprecates wealth nor extols poverty: "You shall rejoice in all the good which YHVH your God has given you" (Deut. 26:11). "Give me neither poverty nor riches; feed me with the food that is needful for me, lest I be full and deny you say, 'Who is YHVH?' or lest I be poor, and steal, and profane the name of my God" (Prov. 30:8,9). One should balance self-interest with social obligation: "If I am not for myself, who will be for me. But if I am only for myself, what am I" (*Aboth* 1:24). Self-imposed poverty is not an ideal; oppressive poverty may distract from God's service: "If there is no flour, there is no Torah" (*Aboth* 3:47).

THE INDIVIDUAL AND SOCIETY

The early Christians expected the world to end and hoped for a speedy deliverance (Mt. 24:3,14,34; I Pet. 4:7; I Cor. 7:25–31). They felt no compulsion to reform a condemned society but awaited redemption "from the present evil age" (Gal. 1:4 6:14). Their hopes were heavenward (Php. 3:20; Heb. 13:14; Jn. 14:2,3; Col. 3:1). Since the world was ending, they were to avoid entanglement with it (Jn. 15:19; II Tim. 2:4; Jas. 4:4; I Jn. 2:15–17. There was no need to resist evil for God would soon make everything right (Mt. 5:39; Jn. 18:36). Personal salvation, not the redemption of society, was the chief concern (I Cor. 2:2; Php. 2:12).

JUDAISM FOCUSES ON THIS LIFE

Although Judaism knows of a "world to come," its *focus* is on this life. The reward for Law-keeping is long life, large progeny, flocks and herds, and an abundant harvest: "If you walk in my statutes and observe my commandments and do them, I will give you your rains in their season and the land shall yield its increase and the trees of the field shall yield their fruit" (Lev. 26:3–5) "He will love you, bless you, and multiply you; he will also bless the fruit of your body and the fruit of your ground, your grain and your wine and your oil, the increase of your cattle and the young of the flock, in the land which he swore to your fathers to give you. You shall be blessed above all peoples; there shall not be male or female barren among you, or among your cattle" (Deut. 7:12-14; 26:9–11; 28:l—14). "My son, do not forget my teaching but let your heart keep my commandments; for length of days and years of life and abundant welfare will they give you…It will be healing to your flesh and refreshment to your bones" (Prov. 3:1,2,8). The emphasis is on *this* life, with its enjoyments and opportunities to serve God: "The dead praise not YHVH, neither any that go down into silence" (Ps. 115:17). "Enjoy life with the wife whom you love, all the days of your vain life which he has given you under the sun, because that is your portion in life and in your toil at which you toil under the sun. Whatever your hand finds to do, do it with your might for there is no work or thought or knowledge or wisdom in Sheol, to which you are going" (Eccl. 9:9,10). "The heavens, the heavens belong to YHVH; but the earth has he given to the children of man" (Ps. 115:16). Messiah's rule is *earthly* (Isa. 2:2, 3; Mic. 4:1,2).

WE CAN HASTEN MESSIAH'S COMING

Judaism does not envisage a world-wide destruction like the flood (Gen. 8:21; 9:11). Society is redeemable (Gen. 4:7) and Messiah's coming is hastened by man's efforts to improve the world. Man is a participant in history not a spectator in a cosmic drama.

MARRIAGE AND FAMILY IN THE CHRISTIAN SCRIPTURES

Believing the end was imminent, Paul advised celibacy: "I think in view of the impending distress it is well for a person to remain as he is…those who marry will have worldly troubles…the appointed time has grown very short…the form of this world is passing away" (I Cor. 7:26–31; cf. Mt. 24:19). Marriage was a concession to human weakness: "It is well for a man not to touch a woman. But because of the temptation to immorality, each man should have his own wife and each woman her own husband…To the unmarried and the widows I say it is well for them to remain single as I do. But if they cannot exercise self-control, they should marry. For it is better to marry than to be aflame with passion…he who marries his betrothed does well; and he who refrains from marriage does better" (I Cor. 7:1,2,8,9,38). John views sexuality and women negatively: "Then I looked, and lo, on Mount Zion stood the Lamb, and with him a hundred and forty-four thousand…It is these who have not defiled themselves with women, for they are virgins" (Rev. 14:l—4). Jesus was "virgin-born" and celibate.

"HE WHO LOVES FATHER OR MOTHER MORE THAN ME IS NOT WORTHY OF ME"

Discipleship preceded family: "Do not think I have come to bring peace on earth, I have not come to bring peace, but a sword. For I have come to set a man against his father, and a daughter against her mother…a man's foes will be those of his own household. He who loves father or mother more than me is not worthy of me…" (Mt. 10:34–37; Lu. 14:26; Mt. 19:29; Mk. 10:29, 30; Lu. 18:29, 30). "While [Jesus] was still speaking to the people, behold, his mother and his brothers stood outside, asking to speak to him. But he replied to the man who told him, 'Who is my mother, and who are my brothers?' And stretching out his hand toward his disciples, he said, 'Here are my mother and my brothers!'" (Mt. 12:46–48). "And as he said this, a woman in the crowd raised her voice and said to him, 'Blessed is the womb that bore you, and the breasts that you sucked!' But he said 'Blessed rather are those who hear the word of God and keep it'" (Lu. 11:27,28). "On the third day there was a marriage at Cana in Galilee, and the mother of Jesus was there. Jesus also was invited to the marriage, with his disciples. When the wine failed, the mother of Jesus said to him, 'They have no wine.' And Jesus said to her, 'O woman, what have you to do with me? My hour has not yet come'" (Jn. 2:1—4). "To another he said, 'Follow me.' But he said, 'Lord, let me first go and bury my father.' But he said to him, 'Let the dead bury their own dead; but as for you, go and proclaim the kingdom of God'" (Lu. 9:59, 60; Mt. 8:21,22).

MARRIAGE AND FAMILY IN JUDAISM

In Judaism, marriage is the natural state and procreation a divine command: "It is not good for man to be alone; I will make him a fitting helper" (Gen. 2:18). "And God blessed them and God said to them, 'Be fruitful and multiply, and fill the earth'" (Gen. 1:28). "Male and female he created them" (Gen. 5:2). God created the earth to be inhabited (Isa. 45:18). "Lo, children are a heritage of YHVH, the fruit of the womb a reward" (Ps. 127:3–5). The family is paramount: "Honor your father and your mother, that your days may be long in the land which YHVH your God gives you" (Exod. 20:12; Deut. 5:16). "Whoever curses his father or his mother shall be put to death" (Exod. 21:17; Lev. 20:9). Messiah makes peace in families: "He will turn the hearts of fathers to their children and the hearts of children to their fathers" (Mal. 4:6). Contrast this with Jesus' statement that his coming would provoke family-strife!

JEWISH MESSIAH REDEEMS SOCIETY

The Jewish Messiah comes *once*, redeeming Israel and the world. Jesus must come *again* to finish his redemptive work . The Jewish Messiah is not prayed to. He does not make atonement; man atones for his own sins through repentance and righteous deeds. The Jewish Messiah redeems society. The Christian Messiah is concerned with individual salvation, is indifferent to society, and is uncritical of Roman tyranny. Jesus said: "My kingdom is not of this world" (Mt. 22:21; Jn. 18:36).

ACCESS TO GOD—IN CHRISTIANITY—IN JUDAISM

Christianity: "He that believes not the son shall not see life" (Jn. 3:36). Jesus is the sole access to God (I Tim. 2:5). There is only one gospel; unbelievers are accursed (I Cor. 16:22; Gal. 1:8).

Judaism: "The righteous gentiles have a share in the world to come. "YHVH is good to *all*...upholds *all* who fall...The eyes of *all* look to you...He satisfies the desire of *every* living thing...YHVH is near to *all* who call upon him...He fulfills the desire of *all* who fear him...He preserves *all* who love him" (Ps. 145). God's goodness embraces *all* people, not only Jews.

SUMMARY

In the Christian Scriptures, the "flesh is weak and sinful." Man cannot save himself. In the Hebrew Scriptures, man was created "in the image of God" and that image was not erased by the sin in Eden (cf. Gen. 1:2; 9:6). Sin is conquerable; its antidote is the Torah, the "Tree of Life." *We* are responsible for our *own* sins. Life and death, good and evil are in our hands. The world is not hostile, with an ever-present "devil-tempter." Nor is it doomed and soon to pass away. Holiness is not through self-denial but through acts of lovingkindness. Health-care is a divine obligation. Marriage is not a concession to human weakness but is man's natural state. Wealth is not evil, poverty is not a virtue. We are to enjoy life's legitimate pleasures. Religion should enhance not impede life. Salvation is not only for "believers," but for the righteous of all nations. *Our* good works hasten Messiah's coming.

The Jewish view of man and society is optimistic. Judaism has faith in man. It does not view God's creation as a failure, needing "corrective measures from above." Judaism encourages moral striving and self-improvement. It does not reject the world because it is evil but seeks to improve it.

*   *   *

The Jewish view of man and society is vastly different from that of Christianity.

CHAPTER 17

ANTI-SEMITISM AND THE CHRISTIAN SCRIPTURES

Seared in this author's childhood memory is the harsh accusation, "You killed our lord!"—my first encounter with anti-Semitism. As a child, these bitter words pained and perplexed me and I was not to fully understand their meaning and origin until years later. Now, when I observe Jews embracing the religion whose sacred scriptures have been the spawning ground of Jew-hatred, I am again pained.

"Anti-Semitism," hostility toward Jews and Judaism, is not a precise term. Arabs also are Semites. Although "anti-Judaism" or "Jew-hatred" would be more accurate, we have retained "anti-Semitism" because of popular usage.

Our premise here is that the seeds of anti-Semitism are contained in the Christian Scriptures. This opinion is shared by many enlightened and courageous Christian Bible scholars and theologians. (See George M. Smiga, *Pain and Polemic*, and his bibliography.) How ironic and tragic, that the book whose central figure is a Jew and who taught his followers to love one another (Jn. 13:34), should became the premier source-book for Jew-hatred!

ANTI-SEMITISM IN MATTHEW, MARK, AND LUKE

Jesus said: "When you give alms, do not sound a trumpet before you, as the hypocrites do in the synagogues and in the streets, that they may be praised by men" (Mt. 6:2). "Beware of the scribes, who like to go about in long robes, and love salutations in the marketplaces and the best seats in the synagogues and the places of honor at feasts, who devour widows' houses and for a pretense make long prayers" (Lu. 20:46; Mk. 12:40). "Beware of the leaven [the teachings] of the Pharisees, which is hypocrisy" (Lu. 12:1; Mt. 16:5-12). How incongruous, these words, coming from one who preached, "Love your enemies…bless those who curse you, pray for those who abuse you…judge not…condemn not…first remove the beam from your own eye, and then you will see clearly to take out the speck in your brother's eye" (Lu. 6:27,37,42)!

Jesus said, "…many will come from east and west and sit at table with Abraham, Isaac, and Jacob in the kingdom of heaven, while the sons of the kingdom [the Jews] will be thrown into the outer darkness" (Mt. 8:10-12; Lu. 13:28-30). "The kingdom of God will be taken from [the Jews] and given to a nation bringing forth the fruits thereof" (Mt. 21:43; cf. 22:14). Passages like these are the basis of "replacement-theology," whereby the Jewish People are disenfranchised and the Church becomes the "Israel of God."

"The Pharisees and Sadducees came, and to test [Jesus] they asked him to show them a sign from heaven…[Jesus said] An evil and adulterous generation seeks for a sign" (Mt. 16:1-4). The Jewish leaders are cast as malevolent and sinister—"An evil and adulterous generation." But more than the Jewish leaders are implied; "generation" includes *all* the Jews living at that time!

"[Jesus] entered the synagogue and a man was there who had a withered hand. And [the Pharisees] watched him to see if he would heal him on the Sabbath, so they could accuse him; and he said to them, 'Is it lawful on the Sabbath to do good or to do harm, to save life or to kill?' But they were silent. And he looked around at them with anger, grieved at their hardness of heart, and said to the man, 'stretch out your hand.' He stretched it out and his hand was restored. The Pharisees went out and immediately held counsel with the Herodians against him, how to destroy him" (Mk. 3:1-6). This is a canard since Jewish law requires that the alleviation of pain and suffering takes precedence over the Sabbath. (Talmud, *Shabbat*, 132; Yoma, 82). This statement, attributed to Jesus, again seems inexplicably out of character with the gentle, loving teacher portrayed as the "son of God." Jesus' characterization of the Jewish leaders as vengeful and murderous, cannot but engender deep hatred toward Jews.

"Then the chief priests and the elders of the people took counsel together to arrest Jesus by stealth and kill him. But they said, 'Not during the [Passover], lest there be a commotion among the people'" (Mt. 26:3-5; Lu. 22:2; cf. 23:10,18,21,23). In Matthew 27, the Jews are depicted as viciously clamoring for Jesus' crucifixion: "Pilate…took water and washed his hands before the crowd, saying, 'I am innocent of this man's blood; see to it yourselves. And all the [Jews] answered, 'His blood be on us and on our children!'" In a similar vein, the Jews are told: "You are the children of them which killed the prophets…that upon you may come all the righteous blood shed upon the earth" (Mt. 23:31,35; Lu. 11:50; 13:34). This convicts the Jews forevermore, strengthening persecutors of Jews down through the ages who believe they are acting as the instruments of God's wrath against the "Jewish infidels."

JOHN'S ANTI-SEMITISM

John is especially virulent against the Jews: "You are of your father the devil and the lusts of your father you will do. He was a murderer from the beginning…" (Jn. 8:44). "And therefore did the Jews persecute Jesus and sought to slay him" (Jn. 5:16,18). "[Jesus] would not go about in Judea because the Jews sought to kill him…Yet for fear of the Jews no one spoke openly of him" (Jn. 7:1,13; cf. 9:22; 19:38; 20:19). "The disciples said to [Jesus], 'Rabbi, the Jews were but now seeking to stone you, and are you going there again?'" (The "Jewish" disciples disassociate themselves from the Jews!). John characterizes the Jews as a synagogue of Satan" (Rev. 2:9). Expressions such as these have fueled Christian anti-Semitism through the ages. John's expression, "the Jews," is a blanket condemnation of the entire Jewish people, belying the claim that the Christian Scriptures is a "Jewish" book, or, for that matter, a "book of love." Loyal Jews would not refer to their countrymen in the third person as "the Jews." If the writer was a Jew, then he was a Jew who had excluded himself from the People Israel. As a "Hebrew-Christian," he certainly does not exemplify the teaching of his "master" to "love your enemies" (Mt. 5: 43-48).

WHO CRUCIFIED JESUS—THE JEWS OR THE ROMANS?

Traditionally, the Church has blamed the Jews for the crucifixion. The Jews, in return, blame the Romans. Most reputable scholars believe the latter for it was the Romans who practiced crucifixion, not the Jews. What is the testimony of the Christian Scriptures?

Matthew: "When morning came, all the chief priests and the elders of the people took counsel against Jesus to put him to death; and they bound him and led him away and delivered him to Pilate the governor…Now at the feast the governor was accustomed to release for the crowd any one prisoner they wanted. And they had then a notorious prisoner called Barabbas. So when they had gathered, Pilate said to them, 'Whom do you want me to release for you, Barabbas or Jesus who is called Christ?' For he knew it was out of envy they had delivered him up. Besides, while he was sitting on the judgment seat, his wife sent word to him, 'Have nothing to do with that righteous man, for I have suffered much over him today in a dream.' Now the chief priests and the elders persuaded the people to ask for Barabbas and destroy Jesus. The governor again said to them, 'Which of the two do you want me to release for you?' And they said, 'Barabbas.' Pilate said to them, 'Then what shall I do with Jesus who is called Christ?' They all said, 'Let him be crucified.' And he said, 'Why, what evil has he done?' But they shouted all the more, 'Let him be crucified.' So when Pilate saw he was gaining nothing, but rather that a riot was beginning, he took water and washed his hands before the crowd, saying, 'I am innocent of this man's blood; see to it yourselves. And all the people answered, 'His blood be on us and our children!'"

Commenting on the crucifixion, S. G. F. Brandon writes: "Jesus of Nazareth was executed by the Roman governmental authorities as a rebel against the Roman suzerainty in Palestine. In the Gospel narratives there is clear evidence of a tendency to shift the responsibility from the Romans to the Jews by representing the destruction of Jesus as initially the work of the Jewish leaders and its ultimate accomplishment as only achieved by their criminal overbearing of the resistance of Pilate to what he knew would be an outrage upon justice. However, despite this tendency, and indeed the more significant because of it, the crucial fact remains uncontested that the fatal sentence was pronounced by the Roman governor and its execution carried out by Roman officials (*The Fall of Jerusalem and the Christian Church* [London: Society for Propagation of Christian Knowledge; 1957], pp. 101 ff.).

Ben Zion Bokser writes: "The Gospels were written after the Church had resigned itself to the Jewish rejection of Christianity and had turned to seek its converts among the Roman pagans. It seemed awkward to missionize the Romans to a faith whose central figure was executed by a Roman procurator. The story was therefore subtly reshaped to minimize the Roman involvement and center the blame on the Jews" (*Judaism and the Christian Predicament* [New York: Alfred A. Knopf, Inc., 1967], pp. 21,22).

PAUL: "TO THE JEWS I BECAME AS A JEW"

Paul faced a dilemma: He sought to wean the Jews from Monotheism and the Mosaic Law and bring them to Christ. But he had to avoid offending them. At times, therefore, he expresses an affinity for Israel. But this was an admitted strategy: "To the Jews I became as a Jew, in order to win Jews. I have become all things to all men, that I might by all means save some" (I Cor. 9:20,22; 10:32). Paul did not think he was deceptive: His intention was to save" his fellow Jews (Rom. 10:1)! But Paul's brand of salvation is "death" for the Jewish people. Jewish converts to Christianity do not have *Jewish* descendants!

PAUL'S CONFLICT

Paul appears selfless when he says: "I have great sorrow and unceasing anguish in my heart. For I could wish I myself were accursed and cut off from Christ for the sake of my brothers, my kinsmen by race" (Rom. 9:1—3). But Paul's intention—much like that of modern "Hebrew-Christian" missionaries—is that he would do almost anything to achieve the conversion of Jews to Christ.

"NOT ALL WHO DESCEND FROM ISRAEL ARE OF ISRAEL"

Paul continues: "They are Israelites, and to them belong the sonship, the glory, the covenants, the giving of the law, the worship, and the promises; to them belong the patriarchs, and of their race, according to the flesh, is the Christ…*But not all who descend from Israel are of Israel*, and not all are children of Abraham because they are his descendants; but through Isaac shall your descendants be named. That is, they which are the children of the flesh, these are not the children of God: but the children of the promise are counted for the seed" (Rom. 9:7,8). It is noteworthy that Paul says "*They,*" and not "*We,*" "are Israelites"? Does this not suggest a later writer putting words in Paul's mouth? In the same vein, Paul says elsewhere: "He is not a Jew which is one outwardly; neither is that circumcision which is outward in the flesh" (Rom. 2:28) To what avail is Paul's praise of Israel when in the next breath he denies that physical descendants of Israel are the children of God! In promulgating the concept of "the Israel of God" (Gal. 6:16)—all true believers are "Israelites"—Paul effectively has written off the natural descendants of Israel. While it is true Jewish tradition regards Gentiles who embrace Judaism as "sons of Abraham," Paul carries this concept too far. Paul continues: "What if God, desiring to show his wrath and to make known his power, has endured with much patience the vessels of wrath made for destruction…" (Rom. 9:22–24). After Paul's mock display of affection and longing for his Jewish brethren, he characterizes them as "vessels of wrath made for destruction"! When Paul says, "All Israel will be saved" (Rom. 11:26), we should not mistake his meaning: "Israel will be saved through *conversion*"! But Israel will *not* be saved, for the path of conversion historically has resulted in the disappearance of the Jew!

"DEICIDE!"

The same Paul who speaks with affection for his countrymen, speaks otherwise to the Thessalonians: "You suffered the same things from your own countrymen as they did from the Jews, who killed both the Lord Jesus and the prophets and drove us out, and displease God and oppose all men by hindering us from speaking to the Gentiles that they may be saved—so always to fill up the measure of their sins. But God's wrath has come upon them at last" (I Thess. 2:14–16)! In accusing "the Jews" of killing Jesus, Paul disassociates himself from his countrymen, indicting an entire people as decides—killers of God!

"WE ARE THE TRUE CIRCUMCISION"

The same Paul who praises the covenants made with the Patriarchs and ancient Israel (Rom. 9:4, 5), elsewhere disparages those who would fulfill the covenant of circumcision: "Look out for the dogs, look out for the evil-workers, look out for those who mutilate the flesh" (Php. 3:2,3). Paul seems to have forgotten that the covenant of circumcision was *perpetual*: "And God said to Abraham, 'As for you, you shall keep my covenant, you and your descendants after you throughout their generations'" (Gen. 17:9-14).

ANTI-SEMITISM IN THE BOOK OF ACTS

Anti-Semitic references appear also in the book of Acts: "Men of Israel, hear these words: Jesus of Nazareth…whom you crucified and killed by the hands of lawless men" (Acts 2:22, 23). "Men of Israel…you denied the Holy and Righteous One, and asked for a murderer to be granted to you, and killed the Author of life" (Acts 3:12,14; 5:30). "You stiff-necked people, uncircumcised in heart and ears, you always resist the Holy Spirit. As your fathers did, so do you. Which of the prophets did not your fathers persecute? And they killed those who announced beforehand the coming of the Righteous One, whom you have now betrayed and murdered" (Acts 7:51,52). Christians who read these words can not but interpret them as an eternal indictment of the Jewish people!

ANTI-SEMITISM BASED ON PREJUDICE

Prejudice is holding negative opinions without just grounds or evidence. It often is influenced by external factors wholly unrelated to reality. It indulges in blanket accusations, indicting whole groups. It loves the word *all*; it judges motives. Jesus said, "Beware of the scribes who like to go about in long robes…" (Lu. 20:46). How absurd this becomes when we find Jesus himself depicted in a long robe (Rev. 1:13), to say nothing of the clergy of Christendom who affect long robes. Condemning the scribes and Pharisees, Jesus said: "They love to pray, standing in the synagogues, that they may be seen of men…*All* their works they do to be seen of men" (Mt. 6:5; 23:5);—another example of blatant prejudice! How strange these words seem in the mouth of one who taught, "Judge not, that you be not judged" (Mt. 7:1); and, "I did not come into the world to judge the world…" (Jn. 3:17; 12:47). Isaiah prophesies that the coming Messiah "will not judge after the sight of his eyes" (Isa. 11:3).

"BUT THE PROPHETS CASTIGATED ISRAEL!"

But, some may protest, the prophets castigated ancient Israel! But the spirit is altogether different. The prophets did not criticize Israel as "outsiders." Moreover, their criticisms invariably concluded with consolation and assurances of God's forgiveness for sincere repentance: "As a man chastens his son, so YHVH your God chastens you" (Deut. 8:5). We have but to compare the Christian Scriptures' censure of the *Jews* with its censure of wayward Christians to note the difference in spirit. As for anti-Semitism—the prophets address their censure toward *ancient Israel*. Modern readers of these accounts do not associate the Israelites with the *Jews* . We believe, therefore, that the seeds of anti-Semitism are to be found, not in the pages of the Hebrew Scriptures, but in the Christian Scriptures.

CHAPTER 18

ISRAEL: THE ETERNAL PEOPLE

Although the Christian Scriptures quote copiously from the Hebrew Scriptures, nearly all the quotations are devoted to supporting the claim that Jesus was the messiah. The countless references to God's covenant with Israel and enduring love for his people are virtually overlooked. Instead, Israel is superseded by the Church: "The kingdom of God will be taken from you [the Jews] and given to a nation bringing forth the fruits thereof" (Mt. 21:43). "Not all who descend from Israel are of Israel…they which are the children of the flesh, these are not the children of God…" (Rom. 9:7,8).

COVENANT WITH ABRAHAM'S DESCENDANTS EVERLASTING

God made an everlasting covenant with Abraham and his descendants, the nation of Israel: "And I will establish my covenant between me and you and your descendants after you throughout their generations for an everlasting covenant" (Gen. 17:7–12; Lev. 26: 40–45). "Oh offspring of Abraham his servant, sons of Jacob, his chosen ones!…He is mindful of his covenant forever, of the word he commanded, for a thousand generations, the covenant he made with Abraham, his sworn promise to Isaac, which he confirmed to Jacob as a statute, to Israel as an everlasting covenant…" (Ps. 105:6, 8–15; Deut. 4:31; Ps. 89:3,4,34-36; Ezek. 16:60-63).

"A PEOPLE FOR HIS OWN POSSESSION"

God lovingly calls Israel his "first-born son, a kingdom of priests, a holy nation, his special possession" "For you are a people holy to YHVH your God. YHVH your God has chosen you to be a people for his own possession, out of all the peoples that are on the face of the earth." (Deut. 7:6,8; Exod . 4:22; 19:5,6; Lev. 20:26; Deut. 4:8,20,37; 9:26,29; 10:15; 14:2; Ps. 28:9; Isa. 47:6). "He will set you high above all nations that he has made, in praise and in fame and in honor…(Deut. 26:18,19). "And all the peoples of the earth shall see that you are called by the name of YHVH" (Deut. 28:10). "YHVH's portion is his people, Jacob his allotted heritage" (Deut. 32:9,43).

"YHVH WILL NOT CAST AWAY HIS PEOPLE"

"YHVH your God is a merciful God; he will not fail you or destroy you or forget the covenant with your fathers which he swore to them" (Deut. 4:31). "YHVH your God will restore your fortunes and have compassion upon you, and he will gather you from all the peoples where YHVH your God scattered you" (Deut. 30:3). "Happy are you, O Israel! Who is like you, a people saved by YHVH, the shield of your help, and the sword of your triumph! Your enemies shall come fawning to you; and you shall tread upon their high places" (Deut. 33:29). "For YHVH will not cast away his people, for his great name's sake, because it has pleased YHVH to make you a people for himself" (I Sam. 12:22). "Forgive your people who have sinned against you…for they are your people, and your heritage…For you separated them from among all the peoples of the earth, to be your heritage" (I Ki. 8:46–53). "And I will for this afflict the descendants of David, but not forever" (I Ki. 11:39).

"YOUR PEOPLE FOREVER"

"And you made your people Israel to be your people forever…Now therefore may it please you to bless the house of your servant, that it may continue forever before you; for what you, O YHVH, have blessed is blessed forever" (I Chron. 17:22, 27).

"HE HAS NOT DEALT SO WITH ANY OTHER NATION"

"He chose David his servant, and took him from the sheepfold; from tending the ewes that had young he brought him to be the shepherd of Jacob his people, of Israel his inheritance" (Ps. 78:71,72). "You forgave the iniquity of your people; you pardoned all their sin" (Ps. 85:2[3]). "I have made a covenant with my chosen one, I have sworn to David my servant; I will establish **your** descendants forever, and build your throne for all generations (Ps. 89:3,4,34–36). "For YHVH will not forsake his people; he will not abandon his heritage" (Ps. 94:14). "Both we and our fathers have sinned…Yet he saved them for his name's sake…He remembered for their sake his covenant, and relented according to the abundance of his steadfast love" (Ps. 106:6,8,45). "He will redeem Israel from all his iniquities" (Ps. 130:8). "YHVH has chosen Zion; he has desired it for his habitation: This is my resting place forever; here I will dwell, for I have desired it" (Ps. 132:13,14). "For YHVH has chosen Jacob for himself, Israel as his own possession" (Ps. 135:4). "He has declared his word to Jacob, his statutes and ordinances to Israel. He has not dealt so with any other nation; they do not know his ordinances" (Ps. 147:19,20).

"JACOB MY SERVANT, ISRAEL WHOM I HAVE CHOSEN"

"YHVH will have compassion on Jacob and will again choose Israel, and will set them in their own land, and aliens will join them and will cleave to the house of Jacob" (Isa. 14:1). "But you, Israel, my servant, Jacob, whom I have chosen, the offspring of Abraham my friend; you whom I took from the ends of the earth, and called from its farthest corners, saying to you, 'You are my servant, I have chosen you and not cast you off'" (Isa. 41:8,9). "But now thus says YHVH, he who created you, O Jacob, he who formed you, O Israel: 'Fear not, for I have redeemed you; I have called you by name, you are mine. Because you are precious in my eyes, and honored, and I love you…I, even I am He who blots out your transgressions for my own sake, and I will not remember your sins'" (Isa. 43:1,4,25). "…Jacob my servant, Israel whom I have chosen. Thus says YHVH who made you, who formed you from the womb and will help you…Remember these things, O Jacob, and Israel, for you are my servant; I formed you, you are my servant; O Israel, you will not be forgotten by me. I have swept away your transgressions like a cloud, and your sins like mist; return to me, for I have redeemed you" (Isa. 44:1,2,21,22). "But Israel is saved by YHVH with everlasting salvation; you shall not be put to shame or confounded to all eternity…In YHVH all the offspring of Israel shall triumph and glory" (Isa. 45:17,25). "Hearken to me, O house of Jacob, all the remnant of the house of Israel, who have been borne by me from your birth, carried from the womb; even to your old age I am He, and to gray hairs I will carry you. I have made and I will bear; I will carry and will save" (Isa. 46:3,4).

"YOU ARE MY SERVANT, ISRAEL, IN WHOM I WILL BE GLORIFIED"

"YHVH called me from the womb, from the body of my mother he named my name…And he said to me, 'You are my servant, Israel, in whom I will be glorified'…But Zion said, YHVH has forsaken me, my Lord has forgotten me. 'Can a woman forget her suckling child, that she should have no compassion on the son of her womb? Even these may forget, yet I will not forget you. Behold, I have graven you on the palms of my hands; your walls are continually before me…All flesh shall know that I am YHVH your Savior, and your Redeemer, the Mighty One of Jacob" (Isa. 49:1, 3,14–16,26). "For a brief moment I forsook you, but with great compassion I will gather you. In overflowing wrath for a moment I hid my face from you, but with everlasting love I will have compassion on you, says YHVH, your Redeemer. For this is like the days of Noah to me: as I swore that the waters of Noah should no more go over the earth, so I have sworn that I will not be angry with you and will not rebuke you. For the mountains may depart and the hills be removed, but my steadfast love shall not depart from you, and my covenant of peace shall not be removed, says YHVH, who has compassion on you…No weapon that is formed against you shall prosper, and every tongue that shall rise up against you, you shall condemn" (Isa. 54:7–10,17). "Behold, you shall call nations that you know not, and nations that knew you not shall run to you, because of YHVH your God, and of the Holy One of Israel, for he has glorified you" (Isa. 55:5). "And as for me, this is my covenant with them, says YHVH: my spirit which is upon you, and my words which I have put in your mouth, shall not depart out of your mouth, or out of the mouth of your children, or out of the mouth of your children's children, says YHVH, from this time forth and forevermore" (Isa. 59:21). "You shall be called the priests of YHVH, men shall speak of you as the ministers of our God; you shall eat the wealth of the nations, and in their riches you shall glory. Instead of your shame you shall have a double portion, instead of dishonor you shall rejoice in your lot…" (Isa. 61:6,7). "For as the new heavens and the new earth which I will make shall remain before me, says YHVH; so shall your descendants and your name remain" (Isa. 66:22).

"I HAVE LOVED YOU WITH AN EVERLASTING LOVE"

"I remember the devotion of your youth, your love as a bride, how you followed me in the wilderness, in a land not sown. Israel was holy to YHVH, the first fruits of his harvest. All who ate of it became guilty; evil came upon them, says YHVH" (Jer. 2:2,3). "For thus says YHVH: When seventy years are completed for

Babylon, I will visit you, and I will fulfill to you my promise and bring you back to this place. For I know the plans I have for you, says YHVH, plans for welfare and not for evil, to give you a future and a hope. Then you will call upon me and come and pray to me, and I will hear you. You will seek me and find me; when you seek me with all your heart, I will be found by you, says YHVH, and I will restore your fortunes and gather you from all the nations and all the places where I have driven you, says YHVH, and I will bring you back to the place from which I sent you into exile" (Jer. 29:10–14). "Fear not, O Jacob my servant, says YHVH, nor be dismayed, O Israel, for lo, I will save you from afar, and your offspring from the land of their captivity. Jacob shall return and have quiet and ease, and none shall make him afraid. For I am with you to save you, says YHVH...I will restore the fortunes of the tents of Jacob, and have compassion on his dwellings; the city shall be rebuilt upon its mound, and the palace shall stand where it used to be...You shall be my people, and I will be your God" (Jer. 30: 10,11,17–22). "I have loved you with an everlasting love; therefore I have continued my faithfulness to you...I am a father to Israel, and Ephraim is my first-born...Is Ephraim my dear Son? Is he my darling child? For as often as I speak against him, I do remember him still. Therefore my heart yearns for him; I will surely have mercy on him, says YHVH...Thus says YHVH, who gives the sun for light by day and the fixed order of the moon and the stars for light by night...If this fixed order departs from before me, says YHVH, then shall the descendants of Israel cease from being a nation before me forever...If the heavens above can be measured, and the foundations of the earth below can be explored, then I will cast off all the descendants of Israel for all that they have done, says YHVH" (Jer. 31:3,9,20,35–37). "I will cleanse them from all the guilt of their sin against me" (Jer. 33:8).

"THEY SHALL BE MY PEOPLE AND I WILL BE THEIR GOD"

"I will give them one heart, and put my spirit within them; I will take the stony heart out of their flesh and give them a heart of flesh, that they may walk in my statutes and keep my ordinances and obey them; and they shall be my people, and I will be their God" (Ezek. 11:19,20) "I will take you from the nations, and gather you from all the countries, and bring you into your own land. I will sprinkle clean water upon you A new heart I will give you, and a new spirit I will put within you...You shall dwell in the land which I gave to your fathers; and you shall be my people, and I will be your God" (Ezek. 36:24–28). "I will save them from all the backslidings in which they have sinned, and will cleanse them; and they shall be my people, and I will be their God. My servant David shall be king over them; and they shall all have one shepherd. They shall follow my ordinances and be careful to observe my statutes. They shall dwell in the land where your fathers dwelt that I gave to my servant Jacob; they and their children and their children's children shall dwell there forever; and David my servant shall be their prince forever. I will make a covenant of peace with them; it shall be an everlasting covenant with them; and I will bless them and multiply them, and will set my sanctuary in the midst of them forevermore. My dwelling place shall be with them; and I will be their God, and they shall be my people. Then the nations will know that I YHVH sanctify Israel, when my sanctuary is in the midst of them forevermore" (Ezek. 37:23–28). "I will restore the fortunes of Jacob, and have mercy upon the whole house of Israel…They shall forget their shame, and all the treachery they have practiced against me, when they dwell securely in their land with none to make them afraid…and I will not hide my face any more from them, when I pour out my Spirit upon the house of Israel, says the Lord GOD" (Ezek. 39:25–29).

"I WILL BETROTH YOU TO ME FOREVER"

"I will betroth you to me forever; I will betroth you to me in righteousness and in justice, in steadfast love, and in mercy. I will betroth you to me in faithfulness; and you shall know YHVH" (Hos. 2:19,20). "How can I give you up, O Ephraim! How can I hand you over, O Israel!…My heart recoils within me, my compassion grows warm and tender. I will not execute my fierce anger, I will not again destroy Ephraim" (Hos. 11:8,9). "You only have I known of all the families of the earth" (Amos) 3:2).

"MY PEOPLE SHALL NEVER AGAIN BE PUT TO SHAME"

"My people shall never again be put to shame. You shall know that I am in the midst of Israel, and that I, YHVH, am your God and there is none else" (Joel 2:26,27).

"OUT OF ZION SHALL GO FORTH THE LAW"

"And it shall come to pass in the latter days that the mountain of the house of YHVH shall be established as the highest of the mountains, and shall be raised up above the hills; and peoples shall flow to it, and many nations shall come, and say: 'Come, let us go up to the mountain of YHVH, to the house of the God of Jacob; that he may teach us his ways and we may walk in his paths.' For out of Zion shall go forth the law, and the word of YHVH from Jerusalem" (Mic. 4:1, 2). "Who is a God like you, pardoning iniquity, and passing over transgression for the remnant of his inheritance? He does not retain his anger forever because he delights in steadfast love. He will again have compassion upon us, he will tread our iniquities under foot. You will cast all our sins into the depths of the sea. You will show faithfulness to Jacob and steadfast love to Abraham as you have sworn to our fathers from the days of old" (Mic. 7:18–20).

YHVH…WILL AGAIN CHOOSE JERUSALEM"

"He who touches you touches the apple of my eye. YHVH will inherit Judah as his portion in the holy land, and will again choose Jerusalem" (Zech. 2:8,12). "Many peoples and strong nations shall come to seek YHVH of hosts in Jerusalem, and to entreat the favor of YHVH…In those days ten men from the nations of every tongue shall take hold of the robe of a Jew, saying, 'Let us go with you, for we have heard that God is with you'" (Zech. 8:20–23). "I will strengthen the house of Judah, and I will save the house of Joseph. I will bring them back because I have compassion on them, and they shall be as though I had not rejected them; for I am YHVH their God and I will answer them" (Zech. 10:6).

"A PEOPLE DWELLING ALONE"

"How can I curse whom God has not cursed? How can I denounce whom YHVH has not denounced? For from the top of the mountains I see him, from the hills I behold him; lo, a people dwelling alone, and not reckoning itself among the nations" (Num. 23:8,9).

ISRAEL, THE COVENANT-PEOPLE—A MAJOR THEME OF SCRIPTURE

God's enduring *covenant* with and love for Israel is a constant theme in the Hebrew Scriptures. This theme, however, is virtually abandoned in the Christian Scriptures, which seem rather to focus on the sins of Israel and God's rejection of them. The message of Hebrew Scripture concerning Israel is one: God made an everlasting covenant with Abraham, Isaac, and Jacob, and their descendants. Though God holds Israel responsible for its conduct, He does not utterly cast them off because of his love for them. Israel is God's "first-born," his "heritage," his "special possession," a "kingdom of priests and a holy nation," "precious in his eyes, "graven on the palms of his hands," the "apple of his eye," "called by his name," eternal as the physical world. Israel is to be restored to Zion, its homeland, and all nations are to flow unto it, to be taught God's law.

ISRAEL NEVER CAST OFF

Israel's enemies like to search among the prophets for instances where God rebukes Israel, concluding from these that God has rejected Israel and turned to the Gentiles! This device is a fallacy. The prophets invariably concluded their rebukes with assurances of God's unfailing love and forgiveness. Whereas the enemies of Israel interpret the suffering of the Jew as evidence of God's rejection, for Jews it as an expression of God's love: "For whom YHVH loves he corrects, even as a father the son in whom he delights" (Prov. 3:12). God warns Israel's detractors: "He who touches you touches the apple of my eye (Zech. 2:8). God punishes his people but never casts them off!

"YOU SIT AND SPEAK AGAINST YOUR BROTHER"

Jews who abandon their heritage often indulge in criticizing the Jewish people to non-Jews. This is an odious practice. The prophets censured Israel, but *never* as *outsiders*! "Love covers all sins" (Prov. 10:12). Those who love their people do not expose their sins to a hateful world. To those who speak ill of their brethren, the Psalmist says: "You sit and speak against your brother; you slander your own mother's son" (Ps. 50:20). Those whose love for their people has grown cold, should heed the Sage's counsel: "A friend loves at all times and a brother is born for adversity" (Prov. 17:17).

Religious groups quote Acts 5:39 to prove they are of God: "If this counsel or this work be of men, it will come to naught. But if it be of God, you can not overthrow it." The Jewish People has survived for 3500 years, having suffered most inhumane persecutions. Who more than the Jews have a right to claim that their miraculous survival proves they are of God"!

God has blessed Israel and his blessing will not be nullified: "So shall my word be that goes forth from my mouth; it shall not return to me empty" (Isa. 55:11).

> *"What You, O YHVH, have blessed, is blessed forever"*
> (I Chron. 17:22,27).

CHAPTER 19

QUOTES FROM "MESSIANIC" LITERATURE

[Following are quotes from "Messianic" literature, with commentary by the author.]

Hebrew Christianity—Arnold G. Fruchtenbaum, 1983.

P. 52: "Do Hebrew-Christians believe differently from Gentile Christians? Regarding the basic doctrines of the Christian faith, the answer is no."

P.55: Isa. 9:6,7, "For a child has been born to us, a son has been given to us, and the government shall be upon his shoulder, and his name shall be called Wonderful, Counselor, Mighty God, Everlasting Father, Prince of Peace. Of the increase of his government and of peace there is no end, upon the throne of David and upon his kingdom, to order it and to establish it, with judgment and with justice, from now and forever. The zeal of YHVH of hosts will do this.'"

"Names are given to him which can only be applicable to God."

[**Comment**: Fruchtenbaum interprets the Isaiah passage as an allusion to the future "messiah Jesus," the supposed second person of the Trinity—"god the son." But what of the "Prince of Peace"? Is that applicable to God? And how does "Everlasting Father" apply to the trinitarian "god the son"? See further on Isa. 9:6,7 below under "D. Chernoff, p. 28," and our discussion in ch. 8, "Messianic Passages."]

P.80: "The basic cause of Jewish suffering is their disobedience to the revealed will of God and unbelief in the person of the Messiah."

[**Comment**: This teaching is one of the prime causes of anti-Semitism, which Fruchtenbaum so passionately claims to fight against! And what of Mt. 5:10, "Blessed are those who are persecuted for righteousness sake"? Fruchtenbaum will probably answer: "Christians have suffered for righteousness sake; Jews have not." But we shall not permit Fruchtenbaum to be the judge as to who suffers for righteousness sake.]

P.107: Missionizing Jews

"There are certain advantages for a Hebrew Christian…in keeping some of the feasts. They are good opportunities to share the faith with unbelieving Jewish people, showing how the particular feast points to the Messiahship of Christ."

[**Comment**: The tactic here is to approach the Jew on familiar ground so he can be more easily enticed. This was Paul's strategy—"becoming all things to all men" I Cor. 9:20]

Messianic Judaism—David Chernoff, 1990

P.2: "Messianic Judaism differs [from normative Judaism] in that we rely totally on the Scriptures" [as opposed to the Talmud and the Rabbis.]

[**Comment**: But "Messianic Jews" have their interpreters just as Jews have theirs.]

P.28: "If Yeshua was the Messiah, why is there no peace in the world? The Messiah was not just to come to bring peace to the whole world. More than half the prophecies about the Messiah speak of his coming and dying for the sins of the world. Many rabbis recognized that the messiah had to suffer and die and rabbinic literature at one time speaks of two Messiahs coming, Messiah Ben-Joseph (the Suffering Messiah) and Messiah Ben-David (the Conquering Messiah)…There are not two Messiahs but one Messiah coming twice—the first time to suffer and die for the sins of the world, and the second time to set up his Kingdom over the world. We are very near the Second Coming of the Messiah Yeshua (Mt. 24:3-21)."

[**Comment**: Chernoff claims that more than half the messianic prophecies speak of the Messiah dying for the sins of the world. We would be interested in seeing all these prophecies. Chernoff says the Messiah at his first coming suffers and dies for the world's sin. Which Messiah is Isa. 9:6,7 talking about? It would seem to be the "first Messiah" because it mentions birth. It further states that the "Prince of Peace" establishes a government of enduring peace—"from *now* and forever" and not in the distant future! There is no mention by Isaiah of suffering or atonement. Is this not the "conquering Messiah ben David" rather than the "suffering Messiah ben Joseph"? Cf. Lu. 1:32, where Jesus is to receive "the throne of David his father." Cf. also v. 54, "He has helped his servant Israel…as he spoke to our fathers, to Abraham and to his posterity forever."—Suffering or conquering Messiah? Where in the Christian Scriptures is the teaching of the "two Messiahs"? Did the early Christians believe Jesus to be "Messiah ben Joseph"? Cf. Mt. 9:27; 15:22; 20:30; Mk. 10:47; Lu. 18:38; Rom. 1:3; Rev. 5:5; 22:16. As for being "near the Second Coming"—after giving the "end-signs" (Mt. 24), Jesus said, "This generation shall not pass away till all these things be fulfilled." Jesus believed the End was imminent. Chernoff says the second coming is near. Jesus and the Apostles said the same!]

Messianic Jewish Manifesto—David Stern, 1988

P.12: "Messianic Judaism is useful for evangelizing Jews. 'Messianic' creates less cognitive dissonance for Jews than 'Christian.'"

[Comment: Easier to entice Jews!]

P.68: TRINITY: "On the one hand Father, Son and Holy Spirit are equal; on the other, the Father is greater than the Son and both are greater than the Holy Spirit."

[Comment: Totally illogical!]

P.97: SACRIFICE: "God's hate for human sacrifice shows all the more how much he loved us; he sacrificed his son despite it."

[Comment: But did *God* sacrifice Jesus? Jesus offered up his own life, Jn 10.15: Eph. 5:2; I Tim. 2:6; Mt. 20:28; Gal. 1:4; Heb. 7:27. And was it a true sacrifice?—"This is the will of him who sent me, that I should lose nothing of all that he has given me, but raise it up at the last day" (Jn. 6:39). Jesus supposedly received his life back again. For a sacrifice to be valid, it must be consumed.]

P.256: "Without Yeshua Jews are destined for eternal destruction."

[Comment: Rather, *with* Jesus, Jews face destruction. Christianity is a spiritual holocaust for Jews. "Hebrew Christians" rarely have Jewish descendants.]

Jewish New Testament Commentary—David Stern, 1992

P.35: Mt. 8:11,12, "The sons of the kingdom [the Jews] will be cast into outer darkness." STERN: "If they fail to heed the warning."

[Comment:—and if they fail to accept Jesus.]

P.245: Acts 7:51, "You stiff-necked people, uncircumcised in heart and ears, you always resist the holy Spirit. As your fathers did, so do you." STERN: "Gentiles cannot call Jews stiffnecked without subjecting themselves to the charge of being anti-Semitic. But Jews can—in intra-family fights, different rules apply."

[Comment: But Christian readers will not perceive this as an "intra-family" fight. Furthermore, the speaker excludes himself from the Jewish people—"As *your* [not "our"] fathers did." This is reminiscent of the "wicked son" of the Passover *hagaddah* who excludes himself from Israel. The Christian Scripture polemic against the Jews is not an "intra-family fight" because a third party is involved: the gentile Church. That the "Messianic Jewish" movement was born of the Church is acknowledged by its spokesmen. The conflict is indeed between non-Jews and Jews.]

P.637: I Thess. 2:14,15, "...the Jews who killed both the lord Jesus and the prophets."

[Comment: Stern apparently is uncomfortable with Paul's remark—as well he should be—and in his translation uses "Judeans" instead of "Jews," to mitigate the anti-Semitic tone.]

P.776: I Jn. 4:12, "No man has ever seen God." STERN: "People saw Yeshua as the Word 'is' God (Jn. 1:1,14.) and yet [John] writes that no one has ever seen God. New Testament faith is not so simplistic as some make it out to be."

[Comment: This is no answer. Stern admits that there is no reconciling the contradiction that Jesus was "god" and that God has never been seen. "Accept it on faith because so it is written!" An example of cognitive dissonance.]

Return of the Remnant—Michael Schiffman, 1992

P.5: "Believer": "This is used instead of *Christian.*"

[Comment: The use of "believer" by "Messianic Jews" underscores a critical difference between Judaism and Christianity. For Jews, *deed* takes precedence over *belief.* In Christianity, the dictum is, "He that believes...shall be saved." In Judaism, the credo is, "We shall *do* and we shall hear" (Exod. 24:7).]

P.64: Rom. 3:21-31, "The law does not change human hearts."

[Comment: Does belief in Jesus Christ? Witness Christian history since Jesus! Cf. Ps. 19:7, "The law of YHVH is perfect, *restoring the* soul."]

Ps. 65: Rom. 10:4, "Christ is the end of the law." "Christ replaces the law as a means to righteousness."

[Comment: But this scheme failed. Belief in Christ is no guarantee of sinlessness. The law is a more reliable way to curb sin—rules vs. vague sentiment!]

P.93: "Messianic Jews have come to their beliefs after re-examining the historical and biblical materials..."

[Comment: With most converts, the "investigation" of Judaism begins *after* conversion. "Believers" usually enter "Messianic Judaism," ignorant of Judaism and in a spirit of rejection of their Jewish heritage. Converts often are disaffected Jews who are critical of the synagogue, rabbis and Jews.

P.94: TRINITY: "A formal trinitarian concept does not exist in the Old Testament…because the revelation of God is progressive.

[**Comment**: "Progressive Revelation" can be an open door for any and every new doctrine if not used judiciously and with Scriptural warrant.]

P.100: TRINITY: "The problem Messianic Jews face is…explaining faith…faith is a mystery. The solution is to affirm that God is One and eternally exists in three persons…without seeking to explain *how* this can be."

[**Comment**: Another open door for doctrinal innovation.]

The Calling—Robert Winer, 1990

P.1: "The number of Messianic Jewish synagogues in the United States alone has risen from seven in 1975 to over 120 at last count."

[**Comment**: Does proliferation prove validity? Many emerging religious groups indulge in numbers-boasting. When they are young and starting, they emphasize biblical passages dealing with a "remnant." When they mature and begin to enjoy substantial increases, passages dealing with large numbers are quoted. This numbers-game strikes us as boastful and juvenile, betraying insecurity.]

THE CRUCIAL ISSUE

The crucial issue between Judaism and Christianity is the PERCEPTION of God. Judaism teaches that God is ONE; Christianity that he is three. Judaism teaches that God is spirit; Christianity, that God became a man. Judaism's most sacred text is the *SHEMA* ("God is one," Deut. 6:5-7). Christianity's is Jn. 1:1,14 ("the word was God"). No matter how passionately trinitarians claim belief in ONE God, the reality is they believe in a tri-une god, in violation of the Sinai commandment: "YOU SHALL HAVE NO OTHER GODS BEFORE ME" (Exod. 20:3).

CHAPTER 20

"BUT HOW DO THEY ANSWER YOU?"

In our classes on Judaism and Christianity, we are often asked: "But how do "Messianic Jews" answer you when confronted with scriptural arguments that seem difficult or impossible to answer?...

"ONE MUST HAVE THE SPIRIT'S ANOINTING"

A typical response we have heard is: "One cannot penetrate the deeper things of God purely on an intellectual level. To understand God's Word, one needs the spirit's anointing" (I Cor. 2:14). Or we might hear the admonition from Matthew: "Unless you become as little children, you cannot enter the kingdom of heaven" (Mt. 18:3). This de-emphasis of the intellect, unfortunately, is a justification for illogical and unscriptural beliefs.

THE "PROGRESSIVE REVELATION" APPROACH

Another technique for handling doctrines difficult to support scripturally is the "progressive revelation" approach. A missionary tract on the Trinity states: "Israel, which was surrounded by idolatrous nations, had to be slowly weaned from polytheism, and gradually introduced to the worship of One God. This was difficult because the Israelites were prone to idolatry, as the golden-calf incident at Sinai demonstrates. A revelation of God's triune nature would have caused confusion. The Israelites were not ready for the mystery of God's triune being. It had to await a later age."

The doctrine of the "tri-une nature of God" still causes confusion.—not among Jews but among Christians! We are reminded of Paul's words, "God is not a God of confusion" (I Cor. 14:33) The missionary tract's explanation is a desperate attempt to compensate for the lack of scriptural support for the Trinity in the Hebrew Scriptures. We do not totally reject "progressive revelation"—if it used judiciously. If we observe *within Scripture* the evolution of a religious concept, we may utilize this method. Religious understanding and practice are developmental, dynamic. For example: In the garden of Eden, man was vegetarian; After the Flood meat was permitted. Children were once punishable for the parents sins (Exod. 20:5; 34:7; Deut. 5:9). Later, one was held responsible for his own sins (Deut. 24:16; Jer. 31:30; Ezek. ch. 18). At first, sacrifice was the norm. Eventually it was replaced by prayer. *But the primal truth of God's uncompromising Unity, taught by Moses and the prophets, remains unchanged.* In this respect, God could say, "I the Lord change not" (Mal. 3:6): 'I may change My program for man but *My nature* remains unaltered.'

We reject the theory that God, in deference to Israel's propensity to polytheism, revealed "partial" truth concerning his nature. God's declaration of His own Unity was unequivocal and attended by dire warnings: "You shall have no other gods before me for I YHVH your God am a jealous God…" Moses was a faithful teacher who instructed Israel as to the true nature of God (Num. 12:7; Deut. 33:4). The revelation of God's nature and will was given as an eternal heritage to the People of Israel and their descendants: "The secret things belong to YHVH our God, but the things revealed belong to us and our children forever to do all the words of this Torah" (Deut. 29:29). The true nature of God's oneness was not kept secret but was revealed to Israel. "For YHVH will not do any thing unless he reveals his secret to his servants the prophets" (Amos 3:7; Deut. 30:12). God's true nature had already been revealed to Abraham, God's friend: "YHVH said, 'shall I hide from Abraham what I am about to do, seeing that Abraham shall become a great and mighty nation, and all the nations of the earth shall bless themselves by him? No, for I have chosen him, that he may charge his children and his household after him to keep the way of YHVH by doing righteousness and justice; so that YHVH may bring to Abraham what he has promised him'" (Gen. 18:17-19). Just as Abraham was chosen to be a great teacher, the People Israel likewise was to be a "light to the nations." To say the Israelites were not ready to be taught the true nature of God is a calumny upon God and Israel.

If the Israelites, who had just emerged from polytheism, were not yet conditioned to accept the "mystery of the Trinity," how were they ready to accept the difficult concept of the one, invisible God?

The Trinity is not a "further revelation of God's nature" but a *distortion* of it. It is an unwarranted and perverse addition to Scripture (Deut. 4:2), contrived by ecclesiastics of the fourth century.

*   *   *

"Messianic Jews" may have answers when challenged scripturally, but their answers must be judged by Hebrew Scripture. The suggestion that Jews cannot understand the "mysteries" of God's revelation because they lack the "spirit's anointing" is self-righteous arrogance. In our discussions, therefore, we shall insist on *Scriptural* verification for all teachings, with careful and thoughtful reference to the original Hebrew and the context. In our desire to know the truth, we shall "seek for her as for silver and search for her as for hid treasures" (Pr. 2:4).

CHAPTER 21

"MAKE US A GOD"

When the Israelites had grown impatient at Moses' descent from Mount Sinai, they demanded of Aaron, the high priest: "Make us a god that shall go before us." We believe that Christianity has, in a parallel fashion, duplicated the sin of the Israelites in its teaching that Jesus was "god manifest in the flesh" (Jn. 1:1,14).

Now, at the conclusion of our study, we wish to re-emphasize the cardinal teaching of Judaism: the belief in the ONE God of Israel, who declared: "…before me no god was formed, nor shall there be any after me. I, even I, am YHVH, and beside me there is no savior" (Isa. 43:10–12).

THE *SHEMA*, KEYSTONE OF THE FAITH OF ISRAEL

As a youth, this author abandoned his ancestral religion and, by God's grace found his way back. He now feels a divine obligation and sacred duty to bear witness to his Jewish brothers and sisters who have embraced Christianity. If there is one, essential element in that faith, it is the uncompromising belief in one, exclusive God. As documented in this book, the Hebrew Scriptures bear unequivocal testimony to this. This faith is proclaimed in Judaism's most sacred credo, the *Shema*: "Hear, O Israel, YHVH is our God, YHVH is one" (Deut. 6:4). Indeed, this declaration occupies a central place in Jewish worship-services. To uphold this belief, many Jews over the centuries were compelled to sacrifice their lives, uttering the *Shema* with their final breath. Would the *Shema* be found on the lips of a dying Hebrew-Christian? Or would his final utterance be, "Lord Jesus, receive my spirit" (Acts 7:59)?

"BUT YESHUA CHANGED MY LIFE!"

In a discussion with a "Messianic Jew," after presenting Scriptural evidence why Jews passionately cling to their faith, we were told: "But Yeshua changed my life! I met him! I cannot deny what has happened to me!" Upon hearing this, I was reminded of the saying: "If your heart does not want...your head will assuredly never make you believe."

We replied: "We do not deny your experience. But you must understand that others with different beliefs have also had valid religious experiences. While *your* experience may have brought you great benefits, it does not necessarily invalidate the belief system of others. Jews also have valid spiritual experiences. You must respect that.

"WALK HUMBLY WITH YOUR GOD"

Humility is a trait of a Godly person (Mic. 6:8). Arrogance and self-righteousness are detested by God (Prov. 6:17; Jas. 4:16; Eccl. 7:16). To claim exclusive access to God, condemning those who do not share our beliefs, smacks of self-righteousness. The "religious experiences" of Jews may not satisfy the criteria of "born-again" believers but they are none the less valid for them. It is unloving and judgmental to discredit them.

THE HIGH PRICE PAID BY "HEBREW-CHRISTIANS"

A Jew whose spiritual hunger has not been satisfied in the familiar environment of his birth-religion and who leaves his ancestral faith may lay claim to an intense conversion-experience, But there is a price: the loss of one's descendants to the Jewish People! "Hebrew Christians," having severed the chain of heritage and tradition, risk not having Jewish grandchildren!

CAN "MESSIANIC JEWS" STAND AT SINAI?

To be a Jew is to be part of a People. Jews have always had to fight for survival. Having existed for thirty-five hundred years, Jews ought to number in the hundreds of millions. Sadly, however, their numbers are small. Every Jew is asked to stand at Sinai with his ancestors who received the Torah—the Law Covenant: "Nor is it with you only that I make this sworn covenant, but with him who is not here with us this day .Beware lest there be among you a man or woman or family or tribe, whose heart turns away this day from YHVH our God to go and serve the gods of those nations; lest there be among you a root bearing poisonous and bitter fruit" (Deut. 29:14–18). We would ask our

"Hebrew-Christian" brothers: Can you stand at Sinai with your ancestors and accept the Law covenant when your belief says you are no longer under the law (Rom. 6:14)? Will you "see children's children"? (Ps. 128:6; Isa. 48:18,19). Will your children and grandchildren stand at *Sinai*—or at *Golgatha*?

"THE OX KNOWS ITS OWNER"

In a radio program, a "Hebrew-Christian" evangelist, inveighing against "faithless Israel," quoted from Isaiah: "The ox knows its owner, and the ass its master's crib; but Israel does not know, my people does not understand...When I looked for it to yield grapes, why did it yield wild grapes?" (Isa. 1:3; 5:4) It is hard to accept criticism from one who has abandoned his people—a criticism which is a justification of his own apostasy. "Jewish" evangelists, who delight in tickling the ears of their listeners by castigating Israel, should heed Balaam's prophecy: "Those who bless you shall be blessed and those who curse you shall be cursed" (Num. 24:9).

In truth, it is the "Hebrew-Christians" who "do not know their owner and their master's crib," for they have left the *ONE* God for a "strange god," a deified man. It is they who have sown "wild grapes," embracing doctrines alien to the prophetic faith of Israel: "They have forsaken me the fountain of living waters, and hewed them out cisterns, broken cisterns, that can hold no water...They have forsaken the covenant of YHVH their God, and worshipped other gods and served them...I had planted you a noble vine, wholly of pure seed. How then have you turned degenerate and become a wild vine?" (Jer. 2:13,21; 22:9). To them the prophet says: "Ask for the old paths, where is the good way, and walk therein and you shall find rest for your souls. But they said, 'we will not walk therein'" (Jer. 6:16).

"I WILL BETROTH YOU TO ME FOREVER"

Israel's relationship with God is like that of a husband and wife: "And in that day, says YHVH, you will call me, 'My husband'...And I will betroth you to me forever...(Hos. 2:16,19). The Israelites were commanded to attach fringes to the corners of their garments "to look upon and remember all the commandments of YHVH, to do them, not to follow after your own heart and your own eyes, after which you go awhoring" (Num. 15:37–39). Succumbing to the allurements of the gods of the pagans was like embracing a harlot. It was an act of unfaithfulness to Israel's covenanted lover: "YHVH was witness to the covenant between you and the wife of your youth, to whom you have been faithless, though she is your companion and your wife by covenant...Let none be faithless to the wife of his youth. For I hate divorce, says YHVH, the God of Israel" (Mal. 2:14-16). "Judah has profaned the sanctuary of YHVH, which he loves, and has married the daughter of a strange god" (Mal. 2:11). Jesus, "god-incarnate," is a "strange god" to the monotheistic faith of Israel. When "Messianic Jews" abandon the Law Covenant for a "new" covenant (Heb. 8:7,13; Gal. 3:24,25), they are "faithless to the wife of their youth." When they abandon the Synagogue for "messianic congregations," they "profane the sanctuary of YHVH which he loves."

"HOW GOODLY ARE YOUR TENTS, O JACOB"

Upon entering the synagogue, a Jew prays: "How goodly are your tents, O Jacob, your tabernacles, O Israel!" (Nu. 24:5). One Passover eve, as we prayed these words, our thoughts were of our "Messianic Jewish" brothers and sisters who, like us, were preparing to celebrate the Passover—in their "messianic" congregations. We felt sadness for those who had forsaken the "goodly tents of Jacob" and dedicated their Passover to a strange god." We prayed for their return to the "tabernacles of Israel," to again worship the God of Abraham, Isaac and Jacob.

A "MESSIANIC" WEDDING

We had occasion to attend a "messianic" wedding which was held in a church. We were surprised that it was not held in a "messianic synagogue"—surprised, but not completely, for we do not believe in the much-touted "Jewishness" of "Messianic" Jews. Yes, there was a *chupah*—a wedding canopy—but how incongruous it was in front of the large, bold cross! The canopy, which *partly* obscured the cross, was symbolic. "Messianic Judaism" attempts to obscure its Christian character but cannot do so completely. Its Christian nature shows through! The bride and groom did not stand *under* the wedding canopy but *in front* of it— more symbolism: Messianic Jews" stand *outside* the House of Israel and do not enter. They affect *symbols* of Judaism but do not enter its *soul*. The ceremony began with the recitation of a *b'racha* (Hebrew blessing). As the blessing was begun, we thought, "Something Jewish!" But, to our dismay, the blessing, though couched in Hebrew, was Christian: "Blessed art thou, O Lord our God…who has sanctified us in the blood of Jesus, the light of the world." We waited in vain for the groom to break the glass, symbolizing Jewish sorrow over the destruction of the Temple and Jerusalem. Instead, the bride and groom partook of Christian Communion! The only *kipah* (Jewish head-covering) in the congregation was ours! We wondered: Will this young couple have Jewish grandchildren?

SINCERITY NOT THE ISSUE

We have met "Messianic Jews" who are unquestionably sincere. But sincerity is not the issue. The ancient Israelites who succumbed to idolatry, may truly have believed in their idols. They derived solace from them, much like the "Messianic Jews" of today, who derive solace from their belief in Jesus. But God warned Israel: "Any one…who separates himself from me, *taking his idols into his heart*…I will set my face against that man (Ezek. 14:1–11; cf. Isa. 44:12-20). Yes, as fervent believers, they 'took their idols into their heart'—they were sincere!

"Messianic Jews" claim to have had "visions"—but may these visions not be the "imagination of their own heart" (Jer. 9:14)? God reproves those "who think to make my people forget my name by their dreams which they tell one another, even as their fathers forgot my name for Baal" (Jer. 23:25–27). And what name is most prominently on the lips of "Messianic Jews" but that of "Yeshua-Jesus"! Thus they cause the name of YHVH to be forgotten, as did the ancient false prophets by their constant mentioning of Baal: "You have forgotten the God of your salvation and have not remembered the Rock of your refuge. Therefore, though you plant pleasant plants and set out slips of a strange god, though you make them grow on the day you plant them, and make them blossom in the morning that you sow; yet the harvest will flee away in a day of grief and incurable pain" (Isa. 17:10,11).

"Messianic Jews" pray in the name of *Yeshua-ha-Mashiach*, rather then "bless themselves by the God of truth" (Isa. 65:16). Moses warned: "Make no mention of the names of other gods" (Exod. 23:13). For Israel there is only one name: "And it shall come to pass, if they will diligently learn the ways of my people, to swear by my name, 'as YHVH lives,' even as they taught my people to swear by Baal, then shall they be built up in the midst of my people" (Jer. 12:16). As long as "Messianic Jews" swear by a strange trinitarian deity, despite their appearance of Jewishness, they have separated themselves from God's covenant people.

"REJOICE IN THE WIFE OF YOUR YOUTH"

Jews who embrace the god of Christianity should search their hearts whether they have been true to their "husband," the God of Israel: "How lovesick is your heart, says YHVH God…Adulterous wife, who receives strangers instead of her husband!" (Ezek. 16:30,32) . Theirs may be a pleasant experience but it is an illicit love-affair with a "strange god." They have gone after their heart and after their eyes (Num. 15:39). They are admonished: "Drink waters from your own cistern…rejoice in the wife of your youth" (Prov. 5:15–20).

"HEBREW CHRISTIANS" DO NOT HAVE JEWISH GRANDCHILDREN

To our Jewish brothers and sisters who have embraced the "strange god" of Christianity we say: Consider the high price you shall have to pay for your illicit love affair. History has proved that Jews who embrace Jesus do not have Jewish descendants. But if you return to the God of Abraham, Isaac, and Jacob, the God of your Covenant, He will again "take delight in prospering you, as he took delight in your fathers, if you obey the voice of YHVH your God, to observe his commandments and his statutes, written in this book of the Torah, if you return to YHVH your God with all your heart and with all your soul" (Deut. 30:9.10).

        *   *   *

This author has spoken the truth boldly and passionately because he loves his people Israel and does not wish their extinction.

BENEDICTION

Hashivenu Avinu l'Toratecha, v'karevenu Malkenu la-avodatecha, v'hachazirenu bi-teshuvah shelema l'fanecha.

"Cause us, O our Father, to return to your Torah, bring us near, O our King, to your service, and restore us in full repentance to your presence." AMEN!

978-0-595-36933-1
0-595-36933-2

Printed in the United States
66757LVS00003B/157

9 780595 369331